Cayman Islands Environment.

History, Politics, Business and Financial Management, Commercial Directories, Education, Society and Customs

Author
Modestus Hopkins

Copyright Notice

Copyright © 2017 Global Print Digital
All Rights Reserved

Digital Management Copyright Notice. This Title is not in public domain, it is copyrighted to the original author, and being published by **Global Print Digital**. No other means of reproducing this title is accepted, and none of its content is editable, neither right to commercialize it is accepted, except with the consent of the author or authorized distributor. You must purchase this Title from a vendor who's right is given to sell it, other sources of purchase are not accepted, and accountable for an action against. We are happy that you understood, and being guided by these terms as you proceed. Thank you

First Printing: 2017.

ISBN: 978-1-912483-39-6

Publisher: Global Print Digital.
Arlington Row, Bibury, Cirencester GL7 5ND
Gloucester
United Kingdom.
Website: www.homeworkoffer.com

Table of Content

Introduction 1
   Government, History & Politics 1

Early Cayman History 3
   1503 to 1670 4
   1700 to 1900 6
   1900 to 1970s 7
   Piracy 9
   Pirates Week in The Cayman Islands 2017 10
   Slavery 11
   The Legal System 13
   The Political System 14
   Relationship with the UK 15

Cayman: A Global Financial Centre 16
   History of Cayman's Financial Services 17
   Cayman Positioned for Growth 19
      Beneficial Ownership 20
      Legislation to Meet Client Needs 21
      BREXIT 22
      Cayman Jurisdiction of Choice 23
   Taxation 24
   Cayman's Financial Performance 27
      Banking Statistics 28
      Investment Funds 29
      Captive Insurance 31
      Reinsurance 32
      Domestic Insurance 33
      Trusts 33
      Collateralised Loan Obligations (CLO) 33
      Companies & Partnerships 34
      Structured Finance 35
   Institutions, Directors & Conferences 35
      Independent Directors Rules 36
      Business Conferences in Cayman 38
      Cayman Finance 39
      Cayman Islands Department of Commerce and Investment (DCI) ... 40

Cayman Islands Stock Exchange (CSX)	40
Ship & Airplane Registration	*41*
Ship Registration	42
Aircraft Registration	44

Cayman's Outlook **46**

Looking Forward to 2017 50
    Health City Cayman Islands 51
    Dart Projects Forum Lane and Kimpton Seafire Resort 52
    Major Capital Developments Government Owen Roberts International Airport Grand Cayman 52
    Stimulating Growth in the Capital 53
    Major Road Work & Expansions 54
    Waste Management 56

Tourism Overview.. 57
    Arnold Palmer Ironwood Golf Resort 61
    Westin Grand Cayman Seven Mile Beach Resort & Spa's Redesign 62
    Margaritaville Resort 64
    The Dart Group 65
    Cayman Brac and Little Cayman 66

Customs, Traditions, Local Festivals & Formalities **68**

The Traditional Cayman Home 69
Backing Sand 70
Catboat Regattas 71
Camping 71
Traditional Industry 74
Attire & Dress Standards 76
Traditional Events, Festivals & Holidays 77
    The Agricultural Show 77
    Cayman Easter 78
    Batabano 79
    Rundown The Play 79
    Halloween in Cayman 80
    Pirates Week 80
    Cayman Christmas 81

Date System 82
Business & Banking Hours 82
Greeting Customs 83

Business **85**

Establishing a Business *85*
    Legal Formalities 86
    Sole Trader 87
    Partnerships 88
    Companies & LLC 90
Trade & Business Licensing *92*
    Incorporation/ Registration 93
        Application Process 94
        Company Registry Fees 95
    Corporate Services 96
    Opening Business Accounts 97
Business Services *99*
    Accounting & Auditing Firms 100
    Attorneys & Law Firms in Cayman 101
    Corporate Service Providers 102
    Business Security 103
    Notary Public/Justice of the Peace 104
    Anti-Business Fraud Hotline 105
    Advertising Agencies & Public Relations Firms 106
Commercial Real Estate *108*
    Commercial Office Space 108
Setting Up an Office *111*
    Office Space Planning & Design 112
    Costs to Prepare Office Space 114
    Fitting Out Your Office 115
    Office Furniture 115
    Telephone & Internet 117
    Networks 119
    Professional Training 120

Education 123
    Schools & Education in Cayman *123*
        Caymanian Children 125
        Expat Children 125
        Reserving a place 126
        Enrolment Age & Requirements 127
        Health Screenings 128
        School Uniforms 130
        School Fees & Scholarships 130

Switching Schools	132
Public Education	*134*
Government Primary Schools	134
Public High Schools	136
Curriculum	137
Public High Schools List	138
Exam Fees	139
Graduation Rules	139
Options for Year 12 Students	141
Literacy in Government Schools	142
Private Education & Courses	*143*
Nurseries & Preschools	143
Kindergarten, Primary & High Schools	156
Home Schooling	*159*
Overseas Education & Boarding Schools	*165*
School Fairs	170

Introduction

Government, History & Politics

The Cayman Islands has a rich history and a vibrant culture that is constantly evolving. Due to its small geographic size, large scale changes in Cayman are felt almost immediately.

So it is not surprising that politics is a hot topic among locals. While Cayman creates its own laws and has its own appointed government officials, the country maintains a strong relationship with the United Kingdom. With May 2017 being an election year for the Cayman Islands, Cayman Resident encourages readers to familiarize themselves with the history of the Islands and how Cayman's government system is structured.

The Cayman Islands moves to a single member constituency this year (one-man-one-vote), so 2017 will be a landmark year for this leading financial hub. Today Cayman may be a sophisticated jurisdiction, but an interesting synopsis of the Islands' humble beginnings can be found by jumping to the Early History page

While Cayman does celebrate Discovery Day, you may be surprised to learn that Christopher Columbus was probably not the first human to discover the country.

Early Cayman History

Historians believe that the Cayman Islands was first frequented by Amerindians, the Caribbean's first peoples who were superb mariners that traversed the entire Caribbean basin and had settlements in Jamaica, Cuba and throughout other parts of the Caribbean and Central America. Christopher Colombus, however, is celebrated as being the first explorer to discover the Cayman Islands on the 10th of May 1503.

While it is likely that the Cayman Islands was first visited by the Amerindians, the Caribbean's first peoples who were superb mariners, for many the written history of the Cayman Islands begins on the 10th of May 1503 when Christopher Columbus' son Ferdinand noted in his journal, "We were in sight of two small low islands filled with tortoises, as was the sea all about."

Columbus named the islands Las Tortugas after the profusion of sea turtles he saw along Cayman's uninhabited shore. Read on to learn about the illustrious history of Cayman's early settlers, who were hardy, ingenious and self-sufficient.

Far from the sophisticated jurisdiction it is today, Cayman's early environment was harsh and quite removed from the comforts of the developed world. But Cayman's first residents not only developed a deep, abiding love for these Islands but with hard work and sacrifice, forged a steady path towards the infrastructural and societal advancements we now enjoy.

Cayman Resident details Cayman's historic highlights spanning from 1503 to the 1970s.

1503 to 1670

When Columbus came upon Cayman, the explorer was on his fourth voyage of discovery when his ships, *"Santiago de Palos"* and *"La Capitana,"* sailed past Cayman Brac and Little Cayman.

The date was the 10th of May 1503, and his son Ferdinand noted in his journal, "We were in sight of two small, low islands, filled with tortoises, as was the sea all about." However, Columbus named the islands 'Las Tortugas' after the large number of sea turtles he saw. Columbus and his men didn't stop. Worm-eaten and leaking badly, their ships laboured on until they had to be beached and eventually abandoned in St. Ann's Bay, Jamaica.

Historians question whether Columbus was really the first European to set eyes on the Cayman Islands; a full year prior to Columbus' journey, the three islands appeared on the 1502 Cantino map. Moreover, Queen Isabella of Spain authorised four other voyages to the New World in 1499. Aside from these facts, even if Columbus was the first European explorer to set foot in Cayman, at the time of his visit, there were as many as a million Carib, Taíno and Arawak Indians (Amerindians) living in the adjacent coastal areas in the region. Archival research suggests that Cayman is a word of Carib-Indian origin (meaning crocodile).

The Caribs and Taíno were proficient mariners, known to make ocean journeys in canoes up to 80ft in length. In Jamaica, thousands of Taíno Indians were living just up wind and up current from Cayman, so it is probable that the Taíno were among Cayman's first visitor.

In 1586, Sir Frances Drake and a fleet of 23 ships stopped in Grand Cayman for two days and recorded that the island was not inhabited, but that there were numerous crocodiles, alligators, iguanas and turtles.

In 1655, Admiral William Penn and General Robert Venables were sent from Britain by Oliver Cromwell, to take Hispaniola island from the Spanish. The so-called "Western Design" failed, as the English did not capture the Spanish stronghold; however, they did manage to seize Jamaica. Shortly afterwards, Cayman became a possession of the Great Britain, following the signing of the Treaty of Madrid in 1670.

1700 to 1900

In the 1700s, permanent settlement of Grand Cayman began with a few families, most notably the Boddens. Between 1734 and 1742, five land grants in Grand Cayman were made by the Governor of Jamaica. At this time, mahogany and logwood were exported to Jamaica.

In 1780, William Eden, a mariner and early English settler, established a cotton and mahogany plantation in Savannah's Pedro bluff, building St. James (now known as Pedro St. James Castle), a remarkable building for that period and the only house on Grand Cayman to survive the devastating hurricane of 1784.

In 1794 the 'Wreck of the Ten Sail' occurred and Cayman's most popular legend (of how Cayman became tax-free) was born. In 1798, the Governor of Jamaica appointed the first magistrate in Cayman.

The 1800s saw the first census (1802) and on the 5th of December 1831, Pedro St. James was the site of a historic meeting of residents who came together to resolve which representatives should be appointed for the five different districts. The meeting allowed for local laws to be formed for better government. Cayman's first elections took place five days later, and on the 31st of December, the first Legislative Assembly met in George Town.

The population at that time was approximately 2,000. Between 1830 and 1840, the first missionaries from the Anglican and Wesleyan churches arrived and the first schools were established (the Mico Charity and the Wesleyan school). In 1835, Governor Sligo of Jamaica landed in Cayman to declare all slaves free, in accordance with the Emancipation Act of 1833. In 1846, the Presbyterian Church was established by the Rev. James Elmslie. In 1898, Frederick Sanguinetti, a British national, was appointed by the Governor of Jamaica as the first Commissioner of the Cayman Islands.

1900 to 1970s

In 1920, a major Education act paved the way for the establishment of government schools in all districts. In 1937, the first cruise ship, the 'Atlantis', visited the Cayman Islands and the beginnings of tourism commenced with the publication of the first tourist booklet.

However, tourism did not really take off until the 1950s when a number of hotels were opened and Grand Cayman's first airfield was built in 1953, replacing the seaplane service that had operated in North Sound since the 1940s. 1953 was significant for two other reasons, including the opening of the first commercial bank (Barclays) and the first hospital (George Town Public Hospital).

In 1959, Cayman received its first written constitution, which also granted the vote to women, and in the same year, Cayman ceased to be a dependency of Jamaica. In 1962, following Jamaica's independence from England, Cayman chose to remain as a Crown Colony.

In 1965, the Mosquito Research Control Unit began operating and also in that year, the Chamber of Commerce, the Caymanian Weekly newspaper (later the Caymanian Compass) began publishing and the Rotary Club of Grand Cayman was chartered. In 1966, landmark legislation was introduced to encourage the banking industry. In 1968, Cayman Airways started flying, and in 1970, the population reached 10,249 with a total of 403 visitors arriving that year.

In 1972, a new constitution was introduced under which Cayman would be governed by a Legislative Assembly, Executive Council and a Governor. In this same year, Cayman introduced its own currency. In

1973, the Bahamas became independent, and Cayman's banking industry took off.

Piracy

By 1660, the English had established themselves in Jamaica and begun treating the Cayman Islands as natural appendages of the larger territory. However, apart from small settlements on Grand Cayman and Little Cayman, most of the three islands were left untouched. This was ideal for pirates, since Cayman also lay astride the route of treasure galleons returning to Spain, laden with gold and silver from the New World.

This promise of capturing Spanish treasure ships on their way home from the Caribbean soon attracted the attention of a motley crowd of buccaneers, pirates and freebooters. The 'Golden Age' of piracy spanned from the 1650s to the 1730s and Cayman's most notorious pirate was Edward Teach, otherwise known as Blackbeard, who frequented the area from 1713 to his death on the 22nd of November 1718.

Despite the celebration of Pirates Week (Cayman's National Festival) at the beginning of November, the piratical part of Cayman history is downplayed in favour of district heritage days. However, some of the biggest names in buccaneering circles, including Lowther, Lowe, Morgan and Blackbeard, prowled the coasts of the Cayman Islands.

According to Neville Williams' 'A History of the Cayman Islands', the abundance of fresh water, turtle meat and wood made Cayman an ideal landing spot. Furthermore, the Islands offered pirate captains the possibility of finding crews to man captured vessels and a quiet location away from the authorities where pirates could hide their loot and careen and repair their vessels.

However, this pirate's haven only lasted for about 110 years; by the 1730s, the scourge of the buccaneers had been largely tamed, if not discouraged by the growing population. If curious to learn more about its swashbuckling history, here is a great article below on Explore Cayman that further explains Cayman Pirates Week.

Pirates Week in The Cayman Islands 2017

Pirates Week 2017 runs from November 9th to 13th 2017. The Sister Islands celebrate either side of those dates.

Every November the Cayman Islands host an annual Pirates Week Festival, complete with a mock-pirate 'invasion' from the sea!

Two old-time sailing vessels, loaded with pirates make a surprise landing at the bowl-shaped George Town harbour with the pirates capturing the Governor.

Thousands of people line the streets to watch the spectacle and its good-natured fun with a new twist every year. Families just love it. It's the only event of its kind in the Caribbean region. The festival then continues all week with parades, costume contests, music, street dancing, competitions, Heritage Days and fireworks.

Over the last 39 years it has become the country's largest celebration, drawing some 35,000 patrons. It now encompasses 32 different events which in the past have included eight street dances, five heritage days, a float parade and landing pageant, firework shows, song contest, two swim meets, a darts tournament, a steel band competition, kids fun day, two teen music nights, an underwater treasure hunt and two running races.

Slavery

The first Cayman land grants by the English Crown were made in 1734 and it is likely that these first settlers brought slaves. The holdings were granted to Campbell, Middleton, Bodden, Spofforth, Foster and Crymble. In 1773, the cartographer George Gauld drew the first map of Grand Cayman for the Royal Navy. He made a note in the margin, marking the population at 400 half free and half slaves.

By 1802, when Edward Corbett did his census, the population of Grand Cayman had grown to 933, of which 545 were slaves. Interestingly, only two of the original founding families (Foster and Bodden) still remain.

It is possible some of these families returned to Jamaica with their slaves having found Cayman unsuitable for planting on a large scale. According to Bertie Ebanks' book 'Cayman Emerges', there were no more than 985 slaves, out of a total population of 2,000, when slavery was officially abolished in 1833, resulting in a ratio of about one slave to one non-slave.

This makes Cayman very unusual compared to other Caribbean islands, particularly Jamaica, where the ratio was 10 slaves to 1 free man at the time of emancipation. In exchange for their freedom, the claims of all the 116 Caymanian slave-owners totalled 447,765 Pounds Sterling.

To this day, Cayman has very good race relations and according to the author Gary Lee Roper, quoting from his book *'Antebellum Slavery'*, "Grand Cayman differs greatly from its neighbour Jamaica, in that there were no large plantations on the three small Cayman Islands, slaves were limited to the trades and domestic arts."

This is part of what differentiates the Cayman Islands from other slave-owning nations in this time period. Although slavery existed in Cayman for about a century, it was not ultimately able to prosper because the main sources of industry on the island were not in areas that were conducive to slave trade, such as farming and agriculture.

The Legal System

The Cayman Islands legal system is based on English common law, with the addition of local statues which have, in many respects, changed and modernised the common law.

The Islands have a good legal and judicial system and are constantly being upgraded to enhance their safety and reputation as a leading financial centre.

The courts system is a simple one, with practice and procedure based on English law. Minor criminal and civil cases are tried by a Stipendiary Magistrate sitting in the Summary Court. All serious crimes and most civil cases, are tried by the Grand Court, presided over by the Chief Justice and Grand Court Judges permanently residing in the Islands. Appeals lie from the Grand Court to the Cayman Islands Court of

Appeal, which sits in Grand Cayman and from there to the Judicial Committee of the Privy Council in England.

New residents, especially those from the US, may be surprised to find that barristers in court wear wigs and gowns.

The Political System

The Cayman Islands is a parliamentary democracy with judicial, executive and legislative branches. Elections take place every four years and the next election in May 2017, will be historic: Cayman voters will vote under a single member constituency called *"One Man, One Vote"* locally.

Prior to this change, Cayman had six multi-member districts. Under this new electoral system the voting districts have been increased to 19, and each district can only have one representative.

Currently, there are only two established political parties: the Cayman Democratic Party (formerly the United Democratic Party) led by McKeeva Bush and the People's Progressive Movement (PPM or Progressives) led by Alden McLaughlin. Prior to the May 2017 elections, the PPM was in power with Alden McLaughlin as the Premier.

From 2013-2017, Cabinet operated as a PPM-led coalition, with the Premier and five ministers being members of the PPM (Moses Kirkconnell, Marco Archer, Kurt Tibbetts, Osborne Bodden and Wayne Panton) and the seventh (Tara Rivers), being an independent and the only woman.

Relationship with the UK

The Cayman Islands have been connected to Great Britain since the signing of the Treaty of Madrid in 1670. From that time until 1962, Cayman was linked to Jamaica as a dependency. In 1962, Jamaica chose to become independent, but the Cayman Islands decided to remain a British colony.

In 2002, the Foreign and Commonwealth Office discontinued the use of the term "Dependent Territory" and the Islands are now called an "Overseas Territory". The Foreign and Commonwealth Office appoints a Governor, whose responsibilities cover a number of areas including: National Security, Foreign Affairs, Police, Immigration, Passport Office, Postal Services and other portfolios such as Broadcasting, District Administration and Civil Service.

Currently, there is very little desire amongst Caymanians for the Islands to become independent.

Cayman: A Global Financial Centre

If you heard Cayman is a "tax haven" you've heard wrong! The Cayman Islands is a well-regulated, tax neutral financial centre. And below, Cayman Resident provides brief summaries on Cayman banking, fund management, captive insurance and trust industries, companies, structured finance, currency and the Cayman Islands Stock Exchange. You can also find out here about Cayman's leading ship and aircraft registries.

As a global hub for capital markets and investments, over the past year the Cayman Islands has remained the leading jurisdiction for international hedge funds, the second largest domicile in the world for captives, the number one domicile for healthcare captives, and a leading jurisdiction for banking, trusts, capital markets and fiduciary services.

In 2015 Cayman's financial services industry was the recipient of a number of prestigious international awards. The Banker Magazine ranked the Cayman Islands, Top Specialized Financial Centre, for the seventh consecutive year. The Cayman Islands was also voted Best Hedge Fund Services Jurisdiction in the 2015 Hedgeweek Global Awards, and at the 2015 US Captive Services Awards, the Cayman Islands was awarded the top prize in the 2015 Offshore Captive Domicile category. Industry awards such as these highlight the jurisdiction's success in striking the right legislative and regulatory balance with the creation of innovative financial solutions for its clients.

History of Cayman's Financial Services

On the dark and moonless night of the 8th of February 1794, a navigational error resulted in ten British ships, including a Royal Navy vessel (HMS Convert), being wrecked on the treacherous coral reefs off East End, Grand Cayman.

Cayman's 'East-Enders' saved everyone aboard the ships, including, so the story goes, a royal prince. When Britain's King George III heard of this act of gallantry, he is said to have decreed that the people of the Cayman Islands should forever be free from taxes and war conscription. There is no doubt that the *Wreck of the Ten Sails* actually took place but there is no documented evidence of the royal decree, however, this has not stopped the story becoming one of Cayman's favourite legends.

The real reason for the Cayman Islands being a tax-free jurisdiction is rather more prosaic. Until the mid 1960s, the population was less than 8,000 and most Caymanians made their living from subsistence farming, fishing, turtling, schooner building and making thatch-rope, while many of the men served as merchant seamen on ocean-going ships, usually flying the American or Liberian flag.

This basically meant that most of the residents in Cayman were living on meagre earnings, there were few companies and capital gains were virtually non-existent, so there was nothing worth taxing. But in 1952, an aircraft runway was constructed and the following year Barclays Bank opened a branch on Grand Cayman. In fact, Cayman's status as an international financial centre derives from the foresight of some early legal practitioners and a receptive Government who, in the mid 1960s, together drafted and enacted legislation to build on this modest beginning and take advantage of the absence of any form of direct taxation on individuals and corporations based on income or wealth.

In the following decades, more international banks were attracted to Cayman, together with law and accounting firms. When the Bahamas became independent from the UK in 1973, a number of expatriate workers from that jurisdiction were attracted to Cayman as a stable place to do business. It is notable that cooperation between the Government and the private sector has continued to this day. This, combined with a policy of welcoming expatriates with special skills to the Islands and a growing population of well-educated Caymanians, has kept Cayman in the forefront of the international financial industry.

At the time of going to press there is no income, inheritance, sales, corporation, capital gains, property or withholding taxes in the Cayman Islands.

Cayman Positioned for Growth

As a global hub for capital markets and investments, over the past year the Cayman Islands has remained the leading jurisdiction for international hedge funds, the second largest domicile in the world for captives, the number one domicile for healthcare captives, and a leading jurisdiction for banking, trusts, capital markets and fiduciary services.

In 2015 Cayman's financial services industry was the recipient of a number of prestigious international awards. *The Banker* magazine ranked the Cayman Islands, Top Specialized Financial Centre, for the seventh consecutive year.

The Cayman Islands was also voted Best Hedge Fund Services Jurisdiction in the 2015 *Hedgeweek Global Awards*, and at the 2015 *US Captive Services Awards*, the Cayman Islands was awarded the top prize in the 2015 *Offshore Captive Domicile* category. Industry awards such as these highlight the jurisdiction's success in striking the right legislative and regulatory balance with the creation of innovative financial solutions for its clients.

With unparalleled market leadership across all the key sectors, open and constructive dialogue between government and industry to drive through new products and positive results on major international tax transparency issues, Cayman's financial services industry is strong and firmly positioned for growth.

Read on more in this section to learn about beneficial ownership, new legislation plus the UK's vote to leave the European Union (**BREXIT**).

Beneficial Ownership

In May 2016 the Cayman Islands Government led discussions with the UK government in regard to the UK government's proposed publicly accessible central register of beneficial ownership information.

Cayman was able to demonstrate to the British government that its system for collecting and sharing beneficial information, via a non-public central platform, only accessible by Cayman law enforcement officials and including verification by licensed corporate service providers, was a substantially better option than the proposed public register.

Cayman agreed to an enhancement to its system which will help the UK law enforcement agencies access that information with the utmost urgency, but in a way that is also appropriate for Cayman and its clients. The British government acknowledged the many steps already taken by the Cayman Islands to implement international automatic exchange of tax information protocols, such as the OECD Common Reporting Standard, and to adopt high standards with regard to tax transparency.

Legislation to Meet Client Needs

Cayman's regulatory framework is continuously enhanced to ensure it meets the needs of licensees and their clients. In addition to legislative changes to allow the funds sector the scope to participate in the EU's AIFMD, Cayman has taken the lead in raising standards of corporate governance across the financial services sector, one of the biggest priorities for global market participants.

Added to the statute books in 2016, a recent example of a new product introduced at the request of US clients has been the Cayman Islands Limited Liability Company (LLC). US clients have long demanded a vehicle more closely aligned with their onshore corporate framework, in particular the Delaware LLC, resulting in widespread applications and increased structuring options for investment funds.

BREXIT

In June 2016, the UK held a referendum where voters indicated that the country should leave the European Union (EU). The referendum vote itself was advisory rather than binding, and the consequences of the vote, and the timing of the next steps, will be determined by the UK Parliament.

Although the Cayman Islands is an overseas territory of the UK, it is not part of the EU. Industry believes there will be no immediate impact on the Cayman Islands as a result of the referendum outcome and is satisfied that its strong working relationship with the UK and business partners in the region will remain the same. Cayman's financial services industry has a proven track record and is strong and resilient and has weathered past global economic change.

The industry will continue to monitor the political and economic situation and plan for the long term to ensure it is prepared for any implications the decision may have over the next few years.

Cayman Jurisdiction of Choice

The Cayman Islands is currently the world's sixth largest international banking centre in terms of both total liabilities and total assets held in financial institutions.

To be successful in this competitive industry requires political and *economic stability*, *tax neutrality*, a responsive legal system, a stable banking environment, a *sound regulatory regime*, absence of exchange controls and the presence of highly sophisticated service providers. All these factors, as well as Cayman's status as an overseas territory of the United Kingdom and its international cooperation regimes in the areas of tax information exchange, regulation and law enforcement, provide the necessary level of confidence to ensure a hospitable financial environment.

Cayman continues to attract service providers such as lawyers, accountants and administrators of the *highest* calibre, making the jurisdiction attractive to foreign investors. The wealth of international expertise available in Cayman is one of the key factors making Cayman a jurisdiction of choice. Clients have access to a wide array of services, including banking, trusts, funds, company management, structured finance, vessel and aircraft registration, insurance and stock exchange listing

Taxation

Cayman is often sited as being a *tax haven*, with all the derogatory associations attached. But the Minister of Finance, the Hon. Wayne Panton reminded the world, in a recent press release in late 2016 following a misleading OxFam report that put Cayman on their worst "tax haven" list, that the country has never had a direct tax system and instead, chose an indirect taxation system that continues to meet the needs of the people.

Furthermore, Cayman has a well regulated financial services industry and is far from being the uncooperative "tax haven" with regards to tax matters or other criminal matters.

In fact, Cayman Finance reported in their 14 December 2016 press release that "international policy makers continue to recognize the vital role the Cayman Islands plays in the global economy as an premier global financial hub." Cayman Finance also confirmed that in 2015, "the World Bank's International Finance Corporation invested more than $400 million in ten different Cayman-based investment vehicles to support critical telecom, energy, agriculture, technology, venture capital and manufacturing development projects in more than 24 developing countries."

Back in 2009, the Cayman Islands were added to the *'white list'* of countries (along with the UK and the USA) using internationally recognised tax standards in their laws (the 'white list' is issued by the Organization for Economic Cooperation and Development or OECD).

The Cayman Islands have been making large efforts to be transparent and to sign laws that benefit foreign governments in the sharing of information and this has paid dividends. In 2000, the Cayman Islands' Government signed up to the OECD's project to eliminate harmful tax practices and joined the Global Forum on Taxation. In 2001, as a demonstration of the OECD commitment, the Cayman Islands signed a tax information exchange agreement with the US which is in force for all civil and criminal matters.

A few years later, the Cayman Islands agreed to implement the European Union Savings Directive, automatically reporting bilaterally to each of the 28 EU member states, interest income earned by EU citizens in Cayman Islands bank accounts. Since then, the Cayman Islands have also signed numerous tax information exchange agreements with G-20 and/or OECD countries modelled on the OECD standard for bilateral tax information exchange and continues to actively negotiate additional agreements.

Currently, Cayman has entered into tax information exchange agreements with 35 countries. Furthermore, the Cayman Islands has pioneered a unilateral mechanism, which provides for precisely the same range of tax information exchange in relation to tax information matters without a bilateral treaty. The Cayman Islands has elected the US Treasury's Model I Intergovernmental Agreement in relation to the Foreign Account Tax Compliance Act (FATCA) to facilitate tax information exchange with the Internal Revenue Service of the USA.

On 15th April 2013, the OECD's Global Forum published Cayman's Phase 2 Peer Review report. This praised the Cayman Islands' "robust and transparent" legal and regulatory regime and confirmed that Cayman has addressed all the recommendations the OECD made in the Phase 1 Peer Review in 2010. It particularly commended Cayman's financial industry for its clear and efficient system for releasing information and noted the quality of Cayman's cooperation and the speed of its responses to exchange of information requests.

The willingness of the Cayman Islands to be an open and cooperative jurisdiction on tax information exchange demonstrates that the label 'tax haven' is somewhat outdated and simply unfair. The professional service providers based in the Cayman Islands prefer (in recognition of the efforts undertaken) that the modern term 'tax neutral jurisdiction' be used.

These efforts on the part of the Cayman Islands have been rewarded by an increase in transactional flows; this is no doubt because of the institutional business which was attracted to the Cayman Islands as a result of its tax neutrality and its improved reputation internationally as a cooperative financial jurisdiction.

Cayman's Financial Performance

In this section we provide details and statistics from the breath of the financial services sector from how many licensed banks and trusts operate in the Cayman Islands to the captive insurance and reinsurance sectors. We also include data on CLOs and the number of registered companies in the Cayman Islands.

The Cayman Islands continues to maintain its position as a leading financial centre, winning numerous prestigious international awards for its services. *The Banker* magazine ranked the country a top Specialized Financial Centre and Cayman was also voted Best Hedge Fund Services Jurisdiction in 2015.

Cayman's positive performance as a global financial hub and its industry awards highlight the jurisdiction's success in striking the right legislative and regulatory balance that is bolstered by the creation of innovative financial solutions for its clients worldwide.

Banking Statistics

Regulated by the Cayman Islands Monetary Authority (CIMA), banking in the Cayman Islands is a major part of Cayman's financial sector, with 196 banks licensed as of the end of June 2015 and the total international (cross-border positions in all currency and domestic positions in foreign currency) assets and liabilities were reported as US$1.399 and US$1.441 trillion respectively in June 2014.

The majority of these Cayman banks are branches, subsidiaries and affiliates of established international financial institutions conducting business in the international markets. More than 80% of those international assets represent inter-bank bookings between onshore banks and their branches, subsidiaries, affiliates and other Cayman Islands' licensed banks.

A testament to the worldwide recognition of the quality of Cayman's financial industry is the fact that over 40 of the world's top 50 banks hold licences in Cayman. The banking sector hires highly skilled professionals and is one of the most prominent employers on the Island. Cayman Islands banks are bound by strict anti-money laundering laws, which together with know-your-customer (KYC) regulations, are recognised as meeting or exceeding those of all major onshore jurisdictions.

The 196 banks licensed in Cayman are split into A and B classes, with the former licence permitting banks to carry out local and international business. There are currently 12 Class A licensed banks in the Cayman Islands, with six of those carrying out retail services. The other banks hold Class B licences and are mainly restricted to offshore transactions with non-residents.

Of the 196 banks licensed in Cayman, 49 are from Europe, 41 from the USA, 23 from the Caribbean and Central America, 23 from Asia and Australia, 19 from Canada and Mexico, 36 from South America and 5 from the Middle East and Africa.

Investment Funds

Since the enactment of the Mutual Funds Law in 1993, the Cayman Islands funds industry has grown from small beginnings, to become the jurisdiction of choice for new fund authorisations by investment managers, representing over US$1.8 trillion in net assets.

Even in these uncertain times, the Cayman Islands funds industry remains robust, not only in terms of new fund formations, but also in net assets held by those funds. At the end of the second quarter of 2015, there were 11,061 funds registered with CIMA (11,010 registered at the end of 2014 and 11,379 registered at the end of 2013).

Approximately 26% of Cayman funds are impacted by the European Union's Alternative Investment Fund Managers Directive (AIFMD). AIFMD requires that EU and non-EU fund managers satisfy specific requirements in marketing or managing alternative investment funds in the EU and came into force in July 2013.

The Cayman Islands has passed the Monetary Authority (Amendment) Law 2013, in order to facilitate the signing of relevant cooperation agreements between CIMA and EU regulators.

On 30th May 2013, the same day that the European Securities and Markets Authority announced that it had approved the co-operation arrangements between all 27 EU securities regulators and authorities from Croatia, Iceland, Liechtenstein and Norway, CIMA confirmed its intention to sign Memoranda of Understanding (MoU) with those same regulators/authorities. The signing of such MoUs is an important step in preserving the Cayman Islands' competitive position as the leading jurisdiction for investment funds. It is not surprising that 85% of the world's hedge funds are domiciled in Cayman.

The success of the Cayman Islands is not due to one factor alone, but to a number, including its reputation, freedom of investment decisions for hedge fund managers, tax-neutral status, highly regarded legal system and the availability of professional service providers. The mutual fund industry is an important part of the Cayman Island's economy, employing hundreds of people directly.

These advantages will ensure that the Cayman Islands will continue to lead the way as the jurisdiction of choice for hedge funds.

Captive Insurance

The year 2015 proved to be another strong year for new licence applications, with 13 new licences issued. The Cayman Islands remain the second largest offshore centre for captive insurance, with a total of 760 companies licensed and is the number one jurisdiction for healthcare captives.

With 246 companies, medical malpractice liability represents 34% of captive licences as of 30th June 2015 and makes up the largest line of business within the insurance sector. The second largest line of business is workers compensation, which accounts for 151 companies.

As of 30th June 2015, total premiums were reported at US$11.8 billion and total assets were reported at US$54 billion.

The most popular region of origin for Cayman captives is North America, with 90% originating there.

Reinsurance

Although the reinsurance industry is relatively small in the Cayman Islands when compared to Bermuda, it does have a significant presence and with the amendments to the Insurance Law, has substantial potential for further growth.

This was recently evidenced by a reinsurance subsidiary of a large New York-based private equity firm taking advantage of the new Insurance Law to migrate from a Class B captive licence to a Class D open-market licence. By drawing a distinction between reinsurance and captive insurance and by offering effective regulation and competitiveness, the Cayman Islands are in a strong position to attract substantial reinsurance business either through new enterprises establishing themselves here or those re-domiciling from elsewhere.

The anticipated benefits to be offered to attract business and personnel to Cayman's shores include "Special Economic Zone Treatment" of reinsurance businesses and their staff. This will mean exemptions from many immigration restrictions and may include guaranteed exclusion from any direct taxation for a substantial period.

Domestic Insurance

The number of Class A insurance companies operating in the Cayman Islands has increased to 29 as of June 2015. The insurance sector in the Cayman Islands remains robust. As of June 2015 the total premiums were reported at US$11.8 billion and the total assets were US$54.5 billion

Trusts

The Cayman Islands are well regarded for instituting a modern and flexible trust regime. The laws and framework governing the establishment and administration of trusts are respected worldwide.

Collateralised Loan Obligations (CLO)

The Cayman Islands is continuing to be the domicile of choice for US CLO managers. CLOs securitize assets, typically leveraged loans, by pooling them together and paying out income and principal repayments from the pool to note holders.

CLO investors buy tranches of a transaction with specific seniority and payout structures hence taking different degrees of risk. Cayman CLOs have made a comeback after the financial crisis as they offer investors the opportunity to access leveraged loans at attractive yields.

As per the CLOser, the Maples group's industry newsletter for the CLO market, approximately 219 deals were priced during 2015, representing US$97.9bn of issuance. This represents the second largest year ever on record for CLO issuance.

Companies & Partnerships

Cayman's Companies Registry (the "Registry") shows a total of 101,430 active companies registered as of 16 June 2016. Company incorporations are a thriving part of Cayman's financial services. Governed by the Companies Law, the Registry also registers limited partnerships and segregated portfolio companies.

There are many highly qualified professional firms licensed to provide company services in the Cayman Islands and the provision of these services is a regulated activity requiring either a Trust licence or a licence under the Companies Management Law.

In addition to incorporation and management of ordinary and exempted companies and the establishment of limited and exempted limited partnerships, these firms provide services such as registered offices, directors, officers and nominee shareholders, as well as the maintenance of corporate records, accounts and financial statements. The Cayman Islands Exempted Limited Partnership Law was enacted on the 2nd July 2014. It introduced changes intended to simplify, clarify and add flexibility to the establishment and ongoing operation of Cayman exempted limited partnerships.

Structured Finance

Several of Cayman's law firms specialise in capital markets and structured finance transactions for international clients.

The Cayman Islands have become one of the world's leading providers of Special Purpose Vehicles (SPVs) for structured finance transactions. The majority of these SPVs purchase groups of loans issued by Main Street US and European banks and re-sell them as a form of investment to institutional investors.

The main attraction of the Cayman Islands for these SPVs, is that Cayman is truly 'tax neutral', so that purchasers of the debt issued by the SPVs can participate regardless of their location, in the knowledge that they will only have a tax liability in their home jurisdiction.

Institutions, Directors & Conferences

Here we give details on what agencies to contact for investment opportunities, which independent directors to contact and which business conferences to attend.

As a global financial centre the Cayman Islands has a number of financial institutions geared towards helping individuals maximise investment opportunities locally, from the Cayman Islands Department of Commerce and Investment to the Cayman Islands Stock Exchange. Cayman Finance is a well known institutions that promotes Cayman financial services overseas.

Another subject covered in this section is Independent Directors who must be licensed by Cayman Islands Monetary Authority and must have insurance with a minimum aggregate cover of $1 million for every claim.

Jump to Business Conferences held in Cayman for a list of events that attracts top industry leaders in finance.

Independent Directors Rules

A growing sector of the Cayman Islands financial services industry is the provision of independent directors. During the recent financial crisis, it became apparent that independent directors from the

Cayman Islands were indispensable when hedge funds were faced with making difficult decisions.

In particular, they ensured that all decisions were made in accordance with the fund documents and that all shareholders were treated fairly. This has not been lost on the institutional investors who are, for the most part, making it one of their investment requirements that there is an independent board of directors. This is also borne out by the 2013 Cayman Islands funds statistics, which show that the vast majority of all new hedge funds have at least a majority of independent directors on their boards.

Effective 4th June 2014 the Cayman Islands Government has approved the Directors Registration and Licensing Law 2014, which requires all directors of mutual funds regulated under the Mutual Funds Law (2013 Revision) and directors of companies registered as excluded persons under the Securities and Investment Business Law (2011 Revision) to register with CIMA. The law provides for the registration and licensing of individuals or companies appointed as directors of Cayman Islands mutual funds and entities carrying out securities investment business, which would include Cayman Islands incorporated or registered investment managers.

The law will require an individual acting as a director on 20 or more entities to apply for a professional director's license unless they meet certain caveats. Professional directors will be required to have insurance with a minimum aggregate cover of $1m and minimum cover of $1m for each and every claim.

Business Conferences in Cayman

Cayman hosts a plethora of notable business and industry conferences throughout the year. These conferences attract a broad cross-section of the professional and business community and well-recognised guest speakers cover local and global events, pertinent financial and political topics and technological advances.

A few of Cayman's premier business conferences include Fidelity's Cayman Business Outlook (CEO) which will be held on February 2nd 2017 at the Kimpton Seafire Resort & Spa and the GAIM Ops Cayman 2017 conference, which is the largest hedge fund operational due diligence, compliance and risk management event, which will be held April 23rd to 26th 2017.

Another major conference is the fourth Cayman Alternative Investment Summit (CAIS), sponsored by KPMG, which is scheduled to take place February 15th to 17th 2017. Other conferences that will be held in 2017 include the 24th Cayman Captive Forum and the 12th Annual Anti-Money Laundering, Compliance and Financial Crime Conference. The globally recognised One Young World Finance Summit took place at the new Kimpton Seafire Resort & Spa on 16th-18th November 2016.

Cayman Finance

Cayman Finance' was formed in 2003 to represent Cayman's financial services sectors and promote it as one of the most successful international financial centres in which to do business.

With a robust reputation for stability and transparency, and a sophisticated infrastructure, the industry is further supported by an impressive list of professionals offering a broad range of services including: investment funds, banking, trusts, insurance, corporate services, directorships and more.

Through cooperation with the Cayman Islands Ministry for Financial Services and engagement with domestic and international leaders, regulators, organisations and the media, Cayman Finance is the trusted voice for the industry, endorsing its integrity and encouraging its sustainable growth.

Cayman Islands Department of Commerce and Investment (DCI)

The Cayman Islands Department of Commerce and Investment (DCI) is the central point for the coordination of resources and information for investors, entrepreneurs and developers seeking business opportunities in the Cayman Islands. DCI also licenses and regulates all trade and businesses in Cayman.

Cayman Islands Stock Exchange (CSX)

CSX, which is a well established and internationally recognised stock exchange, is a member of the Intermarket Surveillance Group, an affiliate member of the International Securities Commission (IOSCO) and has been granted recognised status by the UK HMRC, which enables UK resident investors to receive interest and dividend payments without the deduction of withholding tax.

It provides a specialised and well-regulated listing and trading facility for mutual funds, hedge funds, structured debt securities, Eurobonds, Shariah compliant products, preferred shares, depository receipts, derivative warrants and local and international equity.

On the 25th March 2013, the CSX went live on the Deutsche Boerse XETRA® trading platform. In an effort to encourage potential investors, the CSX will not be charging any trading fees until March 2015. To attract fund listings from other jurisdictions, non-Cayman listing agents may now be appointed.

Ship & Airplane Registration

The Cayman Islands is recognized internationally for both it's well regulated ship and aircraft registries. The shipping and aircraft registries are maintained by the Maritime and Authority of the Cayman Islands and the Civil Aviation Authority of the Cayman Islands respectively. Both organisations adhere to international standards and provide a range of world class services to their clientele.

The Cayman Islands has internationally renowned ship and aircraft registries with a host of legal firms on Grand Cayman that can help you with the registration process.

These registries, maintained by the Maritime and Authority of the Cayman Islands and the Civil Aviation Authority of the Cayman Islands respectively, are used by high net worth individuals internationally plus top companies and organisations from around the world, not only because they meet high standards, but because of the world-class services they provide to their clientele.

Cayman Resident provides an overview on both the Cayman Islands Maritime Authority of the Cayman Islands that manages the shipping registry and Civil Aviation Authority of the Cayman Islands that manages the aircraft registry and what international bodies these organisations comply with. You will also find helpful links to their websites and other salient information.

For information on how to register a ship and/or aircraft in the Cayman Islands and learn about the associated fees incurred in this process, please jump to either the Ship Registration or Aircraft Registration pages.

Ship Registration

The Cayman Islands has a rich seafaring history that goes back more than a century. This tradition is preserved by the Maritime Authority of the Cayman Islands (MACI), which has oversight of Cayman's Shipping Registry. The MACI maintains its headquarters in Grand Cayman and is a first-class international organisation with a world-wide reputation for excellence and efficiency in global shipping. The Registry is staffed by a worldwide team of shipping professionals with many years of experience in the world of international shipping. Read on to learn more.

The Cayman Islands has a seafaring history that goes back more than a century. This tradition is preserved by the Maritime Authority of the Cayman Islands (MACI), which has oversight of the Cayman Registry for ship registration.

The MACI maintains its headquarters in Grand Cayman and is a first-class international organisation with a world-wide reputation for excellence and efficiency in global shipping. The Registry is staffed by a worldwide team of shipping professionals with many years of experience in the world of international shipping.

As a Category One British Registry, the Cayman Registry is qualified to register vessels of all sizes and classes, from yachts to supertankers. In the super yacht range, the Cayman Islands are the world's leading offshore luxury yacht registry.

Cayman also has several law firms that specialise in ship registration, modern maritime legislation (based on UK common law) providing first rate mortgage protection provisions for mortgagees and vessel owners alike, a full range of registration options including full, interim, provisional, under construction and demise charters.

Last but not least, registering your vessel in the Cayman Islands grants you the protection and assistance of the UK Royal Navy, regardless of the location and full British Consular services for all Cayman flagged vessels; yet another added benefit.

Aircraft Registration

The Cayman Islands Aircraft Registry is renowned internationally and provides a system for private individuals or companies to register aircraft in Cayman. Based on UK legislation, the Civil Aviation Authority of the Cayman Islands (CAACI) is responsible for safety oversight and the economic regulation of the aviation industry throughout the Cayman Islands in order to ensure compliance with the recommended practices of the International Civil Aviation Organisation. Read on to learn about the fees associated with aircraft registration.

Aircraft registration in the Cayman Islands is big business with many high net worth individuals choosing Cayman because of its reputable registry. Based on UK legislation, the Civil Aviation Authority of the Cayman Islands (CAACI) maintains Cayman's aircraft registry and is also responsible for safety oversight and the economic regulation of the aviation industry throughout the Cayman Islands in order to ensure compliance with the recommended practices of the International Civil Aviation Organisation.

The Cayman Islands Aircraft Registry provides a system for those persons or companies wishing to register aircraft in Cayman. Based on UK legislation, the Civil Aviation Authority of the Cayman Islands (CAACI) is responsible for safety oversight and the economic regulation of the aviation industry throughout the Cayman Islands in order to ensure compliance with the recommended practices of the International Civil Aviation Organisation.

Any person or company wishing to register an aircraft in the Cayman Islands must meet the exacting standards of the CAACI. As a result of the implementation of the CAACI's high standards and collaborative efforts by law firms and governmental authorities, the Cayman Islands Aircraft Registry has been internationally recognised and respected throughout the aviation industry. For those wishing to get involved with aircraft finance, the Cayman Islands has mortgage regulations (Mortgaging of Aircraft Regulations 1979) that establishes a statutory register for the registration of security interests over aircrafts (or component parts).

Registration fees are contingent upon the weight of the aircraft. Fees for registering an aircraft mortgage vary according to the sum secured by the mortgage and are capped at CI$5,000 (US$6,097.56).

Cayman's Outlook

In this section you'll find a range of 'hot button' topics such as Cayman's rapid infrastructural development and how it is impacting Cayman's environment to discussions on the Island's growing high end hotel offerings along the Seven Mile Beach corridor and the Marine Park expansion. At 'Cayman Resident' we do what we can to offer an unbaised view on changes in Cayman's infrastructural growth and how these changes are impacting residents and influencing the economy.

The Cayman Islands is on the cusp of a remarkable transformation. A paradigm shift that will not only be seen in its infrastructural growth— Esterley Tibbetts highway expansion, rapid development of the Seven Mile Beach (SMB) corridor, redevelopment of the Owen Roberts International Airport but also felt in terms of dollars and cents as the Islands' dynamic business community grows, diversifies and continues to feed the economy.

For the first time in its history, the active companies on Cayman's Company Register exceeded 100,000 in June 2016. This steady growth of registered companies has not been an accident: Cayman's Government, as well as the business community, have all worked hard to nurture its internationally renowned business environment. With new improvements being made to Cayman's business laws including the modernisation of the copyright legislation, Cayman is poised to adapt to the demands of its sophisticated international and local clientele.

With the absence of a development plan, which would have assisted in the *intelligent* growth of our small country, Cayman has struggled to achieve a cohesive architectural vernacular. Some may argue that this lack of homogeneity lends itself to a 'discordant' charm, evidenced in certain parts of George Town where delightful old Cayman-style homes still remain (thankfully) marooned against sleeker new builds.

The SMB corridor is another story. A distinct, unified aesthetic is spreading along this affluent area with the continued expansion of Camana Bay and the Dart Group's other projects such as the Kimpton Seafire Resort & Spa, that opened in November 2016. The hotel has earned a place on Forbes' *"20 Most Anticipated Hotels of 2016"* which won't surprise industry watchers.

The Kimpton occupies some of the most valuable real estate in the Caribbean; since Dart acquired the area surrounding Cayman's Public Beach—once accessed directly by car the organisation has been working to harmonise this flagship project with the larger Camana Bay development. Dart plans to construct Cayman's first vehicular underpass along with pedestrianised walkways that will connect its SMB properties to Camana Bay's town centre. It is anticipated that the associated expansion of the Esterley Tibbetts highway to four lanes will mitigate the bottle neck that often frustrates drivers who travel between West Bay and George Town, as well as help to funnel more traffic into Camana Bay.

Also along the Seven Mile Beach corridor is the new and family-friendly Margaritaville Resort, which will be open in February 2017 and increase room stock on Grand Cayman. Read the Tourism Overview to learn more about this 285-room hotel plus the 50 million dollar upgrade to award-winning Seven Mile Beach property, Westin Grand Cayman Seven Mile Beach Resort and Spa.

Moving south, the construction of Cayman Enterprise City's campus in South Sound will provide a permanent home to Cayman's growing Special Economic Zone that now comprises over 180 unique businesses from tech development to commodities trading. It is likely that the establishment of this campus will further stimulate the already growing residential development of South Sound. And with Cayman's population rising by 3.7% in 2015 to 60,413, developers will no doubt see this growth as another signal to press on with more projects.

But in the midst of all this infrastructural development, will Cayman's unique and fragile environment cope? History has proven that a balance between environmental protection and development has not always been achieved on small islands. After considerable public consultation, Cayman is seeking to expand its existing Marine Parks.

Many believe this is long overdue as the Parks were established in 1986, when the population in Cayman was only at 25,000. Now with the documented decline of fish populations and reef degradation due to overfishing, rapid development, population growth and global environmental stressors such as climate change, Cayman must manage its natural resources carefully particularly with the marine environment being such a draw for tourists visiting the Islands.

But there is good news: there has been a slow-burning green movement sweeping the Islands. Being green isn't just buzz there are more home owners using solar energy to live off the grid in Cayman than ever before. In 2016, a $1.4 million 22-acre solar farm broke ground in Bodden Town, which will feed green energy into the national grid. Reportedly there are more solar farms in the pipeline for 2017 and beyond as Cayman begins to "green-up" their act.

The expansion of the Owen Roberts International Airport (ORIA) is slated for completion in 2018. This massive capital project will result in the country's most important port of call being fully modernised, with new terminals and an expanded arrival and departure lounge to accommodate the growing numbers of visitors to the Islands.

But Cayman's impending transformation does not owe all its credit to infrastructural development and business growth alone. For the first time in history, Caymanians will vote under a single-member constituency in the May 2017 election. This new system will redefine the electoral process in Cayman; and it is expected that with the establishment of 19 voting districts, there will be even more candidates entering the elections race. We wait to see if this increase in choice will result in better overall options for voters.

Looking Forward to 2017

There are major capital developments and big changes in Cayman's infrastructure to look forward to in 2017 from major road works on major highways to the new developments along the Seven Mile Beach corridor and eastern part of Grand Cayman.

Read on to learn about the Cayman Islands national airport, Owen Robert's International Airport, which is undergoing a complete redesign that will maximise the capacity of the existing facility in order to accommodate the growing number of stay-over tourist that are flocking to the Islands.

Other major infrastructural developments that will reshape the country is Grand Cayman's major road works along the Seven Mile Beach corridor and the Linford Pierson Highway. The latter highway will hopefully help to facilitate a better traffic flow into George Town and work in concert with the Government's overall redevelopment plans for Cayman's

Health City Cayman Islands

Health City Cayman Islands continues to expand its services, announcing in early 2016 that a 25 million investment in the facility, will fund two main treatment units.

Health City Cayman Islands will make a $25 million investment in their infrastructure and another $100 million in 2017 and 2018. It was reported in 2016 that these privately sourced funds are to be used to expand the hospital's facilities and to also develop staff housing, a shopping plaza and even a hotel and medical school.

Regarding the expansion of the hospital, a 5,000 square food oncology wing and a 6,000 outpatient wing is planned.

Dart Projects Forum Lane and Kimpton Seafire Resort

With the completion of sleek new commercial builds such as 18 Forum Lane in Camana Bay and Cayman's first boutique hotel, the Kimpton Seafire Resort, the Dart Group continues to be bullish cementing their status as Cayman's most dominant developer.

Ken Dart's projects continue to dominate the infrastructural landscape in the Cayman Islands. The Dart Group's 18 Forum Lane in the Cayman Islands, a smart 85,000sq ft commercial and residential LEED complex in Camana Bay was completed in 2016 and has been welcoming tenants. The Group has continued their work on the redesign of the Public Beach and nearby, the new 265-bed boutique hotel called Kimpton Seafire Resort also opened on 16 November 2016.

It is expected that this $300 million development will generate jobs and strengthen Cayman's high-end tourism product on Seven Mile Beach.

Major Capital Developments Government Owen Roberts International Airport Grand Cayman

The Government unveiled a new concept for Owen Roberts International Airport and has now broken ground on the redevelopment project that started in summer 2016.

Major capital developments are currently underway in Grand Cayman. The expansion of the Owen Roberts International Airport in Grand Cayman is currently underway. The 55-million redesign will greatly maximise the capacity of the existing facility, expanding the square footage from 77,000 to 200,000. This space increase will allow for new arrival and departure halls as well as a new baggage and screening area.

While the runway will not be extended during this redevelopment, it will be reinforced to allow Boeing 777 or other jets in that class to land safely.

Cayman's national airport was designed to accommodate about 500,000 passengers per year but is currently handling double that amount with stay over visitors steadily increasing for the past five years. The first phase of the project is being managed by local construction company Arch & Godfrey. The project is slated to be completed in 2018.

Stimulating Growth in the Capital

Stimulating growth in Cayman's historic capital is still a priority: the Government has assigned a technical team to investigate a holistic revitalisation of the downtown George Town area that will also look carefully at the impact that the Cruise Berthing Facility would have on the area.

Stimulating growth in the capital has been a priority for Cayman's current government. Proposals that deal with changes to traffic and pedestrian flows, beautification, preserving historic areas and landmarks, mixed use commercial and residential developments, will all be carefully examined by the team.

Cayman's once thriving commercial centre has experienced a contraction since 2008. Not only have small business in the capital taken a hit economically, many corporate companies have moved to Class A commercial spaces in Camana Bay and other leading business centres such as Cricket Square, leaving some older commercial buildings in George Town vacant or under occupied.

Major Road Work & Expansions

Major road works are underway to expand two major highways in Grand Cayman. The widening of the Esterley Tibbetts highway into Camana Bay and the Lindford Pierson in George Town highway, will hopefully will ease the traffic congestion and also help to supplement Government's overall revitalisation plans for Cayman's capital.

Major road works along the Seven Mile Beach corridor are transforming the landscape of Grand Cayman. Following the finalisation of the deal between the Dart Group and the National Roads Authority, the Government announced that they will widen the Esterley Tibbetts highway to four lanes. On 9 December 2015, road works commenced and are still in progress. The expansion will extend along the full length of the route, which should alleviate the current congestion between Camana Bay and the Butterfield roundabout (next to A.L. Thompson) once completed.

The cost of this expansion will be borne by Dart and the government, with the latter contributing $8.5 million of public funds. Road works will be managed by the Dart Group. The expansion plans include the creation of a roundabout by Lakeland Villas, allowing motorist access to Cayman International School. Two underpasses will also be developed, green lighting Dart's plans to expand Camana Bay and link its town center to the newly opened Kimpton Seafire Resort as well as other properties along the Seven Mile Beach stretch.

On the other hand, the Government's expansion of the Linford Pierson Highway into George Town has been delayed due to legal challenges with landowners in the area. Some homeowners will have to be relocated by the Government and an Equestrian centre that is located near the highway, is fighting to halt the project. The development of this road was a key project for the PPM-lead government to reduce the amount of congestion coming into George Town.

Waste Management

Another priority for the Cayman Islands' Government, one that is greatly anticipated by the public, is to steer the collection and management of Cayman's garbage and waste towards a modern solid waste management solution that combines recycling at its very heart.

The waste management challenge in Grand Cayman has been a hot button issue for a number of years. But it was reported in October 2016 that the Government had approved a new plan for the development of a waste-to-energy plant at the current George Town landfill on Grand Cayman, putting a lid on a past proposal to close the current dump (aka Mount Trashmore) and develop a new waste management facility in Bodden Town.

Before the new waste manage facility is constructed, the landfill will be capped and all the associated issues mitigated. Along with a new recycling facility planned for the site, officials hope to also put in place a proper waste reduction strategy. This new plan will not only address the current landfill, which has long been a sore subject for residents in Cayman for many years, but will also create a long-term waste management strategy that will accommodate the Island's projected growth.

Tire shredding began at the George Town landfill in March 2017. It is expected that the half a million tires that are currently causing congestion at the landfill will be recycled and used in construction projects on Island. It has been reported that almost 90 percent of the waste the Cayman Islands produces, could be diverted away from the landfill if a proper waste-management system was put in place.

Read more about Cayman's landfill problem in Cayman Resident's Being Green section. This section also has all the locations of all Grand Cayman's recycling drop offs.

Tourism Overview

Both the stay over and cruise tourism sectors are holding steady and with the new room stock in Grand Cayman, plus a new international airport in 2018, we expect to see continued growth beyond 2017.

Based on statistics and collected data, the outlook for the future of the Tourism industry in the Cayman Islands continues to be on an upward swing. Numbers have not looked so promising since 2000!

Projections for the tourism industry continue to look hopeful for 2017, particularly when we look at air arrivals for 2016 which were at 385,451. Stay over tourist numbers fell only slightly in 2016 (1.41%), compared to 2015 but a half year report by the Cayman Island Department of Tourism (2016) detailed that tourist were highly satisfied with their visit to the Cayman Islands. Over 96.5 percent of the tourist surveyed reported that they would travel to the Cayman Islands again (by air).

And those repeat visitors to Cayman will have even more to look forward to in 2017 and beyond. Recently, the choices for stay over tourist in Grand Cayman have diversified, with the Kimpton Seafire Resort providing Cayman's first sleek "boutique" hotel experience to the new Margaritaville Resort bringing Jimmy Buffet-style family fun to Seven Mile Beach. The 50 million dollar redesign of the renowned Westin Grand Cayman Seven Mile Beach Resort & Spa is also wowing visitors. This increase in room stock and services in Grand Cayman, coupled with dozens of planned residential developments for the Seven Mile Beach corridor and the Island's other coastal hot spots to the east, will solidify the Cayman Islands as one of the premier destinations in Western Hemisphere for sand, sea and sun lovers.

According to the World Tourism Organization (2016 Tourism Highlights), the Caribbean is one of the best performing regions, reporting a 7% growth in international arrivals, followed closely by North America that reported a 6% growth. This upward trend is undoubtedly consistent with with the current consumer confidence in the United States and of course, it also points to the overall desirability of the Caribbean region.

The Cayman Islands Department of Tourism reported that visitors from the Northeast region of the United States are the primary market; however, arrivals from Canada and Europe have been steady. It is not surprising that the government continues to push the *Caymankind* brand in major cities around the world as nearly 80 percent of stay over visitors that travel to the Island, come for recreational purposes such as swimming at Seven Mile Beach and diving. The largest demographic group that visits Cayman consists of males and females from North America between the ages of 36 and 49.

Cruise ship numbers continue to also be high and only dipped slightly in 2016. The Cayman Islands Port Authority reported that a total of

1,711,853 cruise ship passengers travelled to Grand Cayman in 2016. (1,716,812 arrived in 2015.) Remarkably, Cayman still enjoys record high cruise ship visitations (since 2000) and all without a cruise berthing facility.

Currently, cruise ships use local tenders some of the best in the region to transport passengers to shore and this process usually runs smoothly. Debate still continues as to the necessity and viability of constructing a cruise berthing facility, construction of which opponents fear will have a long-term environmental impact that outweighs any possible economic benefits. Some proponents however, believe that a proper docking facility would stimulate growth on the waterfront, allowing tourists more flexibility to disembark.

This is an election year for the Cayman Islands, so industry watchers will await the outcome of May 2017 to determine if present plans for a berthing facility, will eventually become a reality in the coming years. Cayman is one of the Caribbean's world class destinations not only because of its well developed infrastructure and sophisticated services, but also for its natural beauty. So, it is only reasonable to expect that any large scale development will be measured and thoughtful, so that the natural beauty that brings people these shores is preserved.

Arnold Palmer Ironwood Golf Resort

The Arnold Palmer-branded Ironwood Golf Lodge, a multi-million dollar development project set for Cayman's eastern districts, has been in the works for a few years. The project was contingent on a number of issues being resolved, one being that road access to the development encroached on the Cayman National Trust's heritage site, the Mastic Trail. This trail that is visited by tourist and locals annually is of significant importance to the Cayman Islands; it is one of the last remaining dry wood forests in the country where a variety of rare species of flora and fauna can be found. An agreement was reached in 2014 by the Government and the National Trust to divert the access road away from sensitive ecological areas in the wetlands and Mastic Trail.

But one issue that is still pending is the actual construction of the 10-mile extension east-west arterial highway that will allow a quicker and more direct route to the future development from George Town. Government's anticipated support of the project involved agreeing to contribute to funding and building this highway. But currently, it remains unknown when road works will actually commense.

In late 2016, well known Cayman developer Joe Imparato announced that he would design and build the clubhouse and lodge for the development. He also explained that two five-story buildings for a hotel and the residences were in the works. The clubhouse and lodge is slated for completion in late 2018.

Although legend Arnold Palmer died in September of 2016, he was highly supportive of the project and his family is still currently involved.

Westin Grand Cayman Seven Mile Beach Resort & Spa's Redesign

As we mentioned in the overview, Grand Cayman's stay over tourist have much to look forward to in 2017. The discerning traveller should have another Cayman property on their radar. Westin Grand Cayman Seven Mile Beach Resort & Spa's extensive $50 million redesign is nearing completion (mid 2017) with the first phase already done.

One of Condé Nast's Traveller World's Best Caribbean Resorts (2016), the Westin Grand Cayman is not only renowned for offering guest superior room stock and services, but also one of the widest and most expansive stretches of Cayman's famed Seven Mile Beach. Today, the property provides even more to travelers seeking a sophisticated beach-side experience in Cayman.

Guests that arrive at the Westin Grand Cayman will be now welcomed in their chic new lobby with sand-tone wood flooring and organic columns, with sweeping views of the Caribbean Sea. They can also sip on a fresh cocktail at the lobby's new Catboat Lobby Bar before venturing out to the beach or to the expanded freshwater pool and swim up bar, considered one of the largest in Grand Cayman. There is even a call-waiting button to summon a server at the pool deck.

Along with the fine dining experiences found at Beach Houseand the other restaurants on this 8-acre property, visitors can pop over for a snack at the new cafe: Cayman Coffee Exchangeor work on their New Year resolutions at the hotel's fitness centre. A bit of pampering at the Hibiscus Spa is always a treat for both visitors and locals alike.

We hear the Westin Grand Cayman's live entertainment options are even bigger and better too. The second phase of the hotel's transformation (May-August 2017) will include full renovations to guest rooms and suites.

The Marriott Redevelopment

Proving that confidence continues to be high in projections for an increase in future stay-over visitors, the Grand Cayman Marriott Beach Resort completed a 16 million dollar redevelopment in 2014, introducing their "Beach House" concept to Grand Cayman.

The hotel's decor could be described as relaxed elegance and the new restaurants on the property centre on fresh local produce and seafood, and high end culinary offerings. Making waves with foodies is the restaurant Anchor and Den, which opened in the hotel's lobby in 2014.

The hotel went up for sale in late January 2015, and many real estate watchers estimate it will sell in excess of $100 million. (It has been confirmed that the Marriott will continue to manage the hotel after the sale.)

Margaritaville Resort

Margaritaville Resort is coming to Seven Mile Beach! The old and somewhat faded Treasure Island hotel will get a new lease on life when it is transformed into a Margaritaville resort in February 2017. What's more, this highly anticipated resort is already taking reservations! Occupying prime real estate on Cayman's own "gold coast" Seven Mile Beach, the 285-room hotel will boost multiple restaurants and bars, several swimming pools (including a two-story pool slide), retail shops, a dedicated kid's zone, a 24-hour fitness centre, plus a meeting and event centre.

(Steak lovers should check out the Resort's new hotspot YARA that will feature classic Wagyu steaks and Niaman Ranch lamb along with an extensive raw bar and wine list.)

The Howard Hospitality Group purchased the property in late 2015 and announced their redevelopment plans shortly after. Renovation of the 110 condo suites on the property are also slated to begin this year.

The Dart Group

The Dart Group continues to be bullish, given their recent acquisitions and their big reveal in 2015 that they will inject $300 million into Camana Bay to expand the development.

This expansion plan includes the construction of an underpass on West Bay Road and the widening of the Esterley Tibbetts Highway; the latter will be a four lane highway and road works will continue throughout 2017. The Group's overall plan also calls for the creation of pedestrianized and vehicular links that connect Camana Bay to other key Dart properties—The Kimpton and possibly the Cayman Islands Yacht Club—along the Seven Mile Beach strip, achieving their larger vision: "sea to Sound connectivity".

This plan, however, is simply just the first phase in the Group's ambitious 10-year development plan that was quietly revealed at a private symposium hosted by Ernst and Young in 2014. It was reported in 2015 that the Dart Group had purchased seaside properties in East End, including the unmarred Barefoot Beach.

To date, it is unknown if the Group plans to develop this picturesque stretch of beach that is much beloved by locals and visitors to Grand Cayman.

Cayman Brac and Little Cayman

Cayman Brac and Little Cayman will have a decidedly different outlook than Grand Cayman. While development along Grand Cayman's renowned Seven Mile Beach corridor remains robust, the Government has promised to keep the charm of the Sister Islands intake; residents and return visitors flock to these Islands for a more tranquil and eco-friendly experience.

Stakeholders and conservationist are hopeful that unsuitable developments, that would mar that experience, will be avoided given what is happening in tiny Bimini (Bahamas) after the development of the Bimini Bay Resort. The recent construction of the 10,000 square foot casino and a 343-room hotel and marina has angered many locals, as large scale developments such as these are changing the face of one of the Bahamas' most treasured Out Islands.

In early June 2016, it was announced that the Dart Group had acquired Paradise Villas resort and the Hungry Iguana restaurant in Little Cayman. No immediate redevelopment plans were revealed, but CEO of Dart Realty Mark VanDevlde maintains that the Group is committed to preserving the unique characteristics of Little Cayman.

Customs, Traditions, Local Festivals & Formalities

Once known as the "islands time forgot," the Cayman Islands have been catapulted into the 21st century at, some say, an alarming rate. In spite of the Island's rapid development, many deep rooted customs and traditions still play a part in day-to-day Cayman life.

Interestingly, the last decade has seen a determined effort to maintain the delicate balance between preserving the essence and simplicity of the Cayman Islands' past while moving resolutely into the future to maintain the country's status as one of the world's premier tourism, banking and finance centers.

Many Caymanian customs and traditions are linked inextricably to religious holidays. Whether camping by the sea at Easter or hunting for land crabs during the rainy season, these events are social in nature and family-oriented. Visit East End on any given Sunday and you will see families and friends, recently returned from church, 'shooting the breeze' on their front porches or enjoying a noisy game of dominoes under the shade of a breadfruit tree (what's 'breadfruit' you ask? There's a great local food glossary on Cayman Good Taste!).

Being up on the 'Marl Road' (local gossip) for some, is as important as drawing breath! And if you want to sound like you're really in the know, never, ever refer to the Cayman Islands as 'the Caymans'! We simply say CayMAN as in... "aren't you lucky to live in Cayman." Also, don't leave without finding out about Cayman's colourful carnival Batabano plus other local festivals.

The Traditional Cayman Home

The oldest known style of Caymanian home is the 'wattle and daub' cottage, which dates back to the mid-18th century. The house was usually rectangular, with foundation posts made from termite-resistant ironwood.

Gaps between the ironwood or mahogany posts in this Cayman dwelling were filled with a basket weave of wattled sticks and then plastered on either side with lime daub made from burnt coral. The earliest roofs were thatched using palm tree fronds, but in more recent times, wood, shingle or corrugated zinc has been used.

Windows were simple openings with wood board shutters, while smoke-pots helped keep out mosquitoes.

Normally, these one-storey dwellings would feature a steeply pitched roof. This would keep the houses cooler as hot air rises. The typical yard would have been shaded with seagrape and popnut trees, and there would be a separate 'caboose' for cooking.

Although modest in terms of aesthetics, these traditional homes tended to be very strong and resilient during storms. Sadly most Cayman's old wattle and daub homes no longer exist due to development, but the Cayman Islands National Museum has a fascinating wattle and daub exhibit at their historic building.

Backing Sand

Family outings to the beach on the weekend are a major part of Caymanian culture, but sand plays another very important role in Cayman at Christmas time.

Unlike many parents around the world, Caymanians have always been able to guarantee their children a white Christmas. The tradition of 'backing sand' has stood the test of time.

Often, beginning as early as October, Caymanian women and children could be seen by the light of the moon carrying 'ground baskets,' woven from leaves of the magnificent thatch palm trees that tower loftily over the islands, brimming with powder-white sand from the beaches. The sand would be deposited in the front yard and on Christmas Eve raked into intricate patterns and decorated with shiny new conch shell pathways.

Catboat Regattas

Cayman's proud maritime history has served to provide many lasting traditions. The Catboat, a simple but highly maneuverable sailing boat once used for fishing and turtling in and around Cayman waters, is enjoying a revival thanks to the efforts of the Cayman Islands Catboat Club.

Regular regattas are held in Grand Cayman and the sight of these small, skillfully crafted vessels tacking their way around George Town's bustling harbour, vying for space amid cruise ships, dive boats and tenders, is a truly remarkable snapshot of the juxtaposition of past and present in Cayman.

Camping

Camping by the sea at Easter is a long-held Caymanian tradition. Popular spots to camp are beaches along the Queen's Highway, around Rum Point and Cayman Kai, as well as Seven Mile Beach.

Every year you will see hundreds, if not thousands of people camp on beaches all over the Cayman Islands. It's a great opportunity for families and friends to get together and reminisce about simpler times, as well as enjoy the natural beauty of the Cayman coastline.

Popular camping spots in Grand Cayman are beaches along the Queen's Highway in East End, in and around Rum Point and Cayman Kai and along Seven Mile Beach. However, on the latter it is always private, undeveloped land or one of the public beaches that you can camp on. A favourite spot in Little Cayman is Point of Sand.

The perception to date has been that the police quietly overlook people camping and that at any other time of the year it is illegal. However, it is in fact legal! There are a few very specific rules however, that must be observed to make it legal. These are as follows:

- ✓ If you camp on a privately owned piece of land then all garbage that you generate must be taken away with you when you leave. If you camp on a public beach then you must ensure that your garbage is put in the bins or if there is no bin (or it is full) then you take the garbage away with you and dispose of it properly somewhere else.

- ✓ There is a legal requirement for human waste to be disposed of properly. Therefore you must either rent a portaloo or camp near a public toilet.

- ✓ You are allowed to camp on the Government's public beaches but you cannot camp on land which has a "Do Not Trespass" sign on it, or on land which has a private property sign and the owner has not given you permission to camp there.

- ✓ You can reserve a cabana on one of the public beaches by calling the Recreation, Parks & Cemeteries Unit (Tel: 345 946-8250. There is no charge.

- ✓ Lighting a bonfire is illegal unless permission is gained from a) the Department of Environmental Health (345 949-6696) and the Fire Department (345 949-2276). You should allow two weeks notice and there may be a charge of CI$25. Keep bonfires away from trees and bushes. Make sure ashes are extinguished with water and that they are not smouldering when you leave the camp site.

- ✓ If you light a fire or have a propane BBQ then the proper equipment must be used to prevent injuries.

- ✓ All bonfires/cooking fires must be covered properly (i.e. buried as deep as possible) after you have finished with it to prevent anyone stumbling into it by mistake and getting burned.
- ✓ Importing tents and camp beds is allowed.

Traditional Industry

Long before tourism and the financial services powered Cayman financially, the principle economic mainstay of the Cayman Islands was turtling. Locals ate and sold the meat and exported the large shells overseas so it that it could be used in finished goods that were sold in Europe.

However, there have been other industries, including schooner building, sponge harvesting, the gathering of seabird eggs, wrecking, guano collecting, catching sharks for the leather industry, the felling and removal of hardwoods such as mahogany and cedar, the barking of red mangrove trees and cutting of logwood for their use in dyes. Coconuts were exported, cotton was gathered, ropes were made from thatch and, for a period, Caymanians worked as merchant seamen on commercial ships. But compared to turtling, all of these industries were of a comparatively short duration.

Thatch Weaving & Rope Making Another noteworthy tradition is that of thatch weaving. 'Laying rope' was once one of the few means of making a living for Caymanian women and children while the men were away at sea and this valuable custom has been passed down from generation to generation. Certain districts were known to produce the best 'tops' for cutting and people would often walk for miles to collect bundles of thatch, which would later be stripped, dried and twisted into fine fathoms of rope. These, in turn, would be traded overseas or exchanged for goods such as cloth, sugar or kerosene.

Turtling and Cayman's Turtle Industry When the first Europeans came to Cayman they found one of the largest turtle nesting grounds on earth. For nearly 200 years, ships of all nations (particularly French, Dutch and English) came to these shores to 'turn' green and loggerhead turtles and dry their flesh, an easily obtainable source of protein for ship or plantation stores. Early on, Cayman became the centre of the Caribbean turtle industry. The English from Jamaica, who first settled in Cayman in the 1660s, came to be regarded as skilled turtlers. By 1800, the turtle population had dwindled and the local turtling fleet turned their attention to the south coast of Cuba and the coastline of Central America.

Until the early 1960s, Cayman still supplied the largest share of turtles entering foreign markets from the Caribbean. These were mostly caught on the Mosquito Coast of Nicaragua. Turtle hunting was officially banned in 1988, however, in honour of Cayman's turtling heritage, certain individuals are permitted to hunt turtles under license in accordance with the Marine Conservation Law. While typically some of these individuals apply to renew their licenses annually, in the past few years, no turtles have been taken under a license.

Additionally, the Cayman Turtle Centre is a major tourist attraction and continues to supply the local market with turtle meat.

Attire & Dress Standards

Residents in the Cayman Islands are generally a fashionably casual bunch. But during the work-week men who are business professionals may wear long trousers, long sleeved collared shirts and a tie. Jackets are very rarely worn, even in board meetings but are compulsory for lawyers attending court proceedings. You may see women in Cayman wearing a smart skirt, dress or slacks with a blouse at the office - all very appropriate for a professional setting.

For social occasions, Cayman residents love to dress up and casual attire will be quite smart. Women dress in the same way they would in

America and Europe. Away from the workplace, the dress is casual shopping and running errands are done in whatever is cool.

In the Cayman Islands shorts, T-shirts and sundresses are acceptable but only tourists wear swimwear away from the beach. Some business establishments such as supermarkets may require patrons to wear t-shirts (or an appropriate swimsuit cover) and shoes.

Traditional Events, Festivals & Holidays

From the highly anticipated Pirates Week and Batabano (Cayman's annual carnival) to the popular local play Rundown, there are a host of traditional events, festivals and holidays that make the Cayman Islands especially unique and of course a fabulous place to call home

Throughout the entire year, the Cayman Islands will wow you with festive holidays, traditional events and massively attended, internationally renowned festivals unique to the country.

The Agricultural Show

Early Caymanians supplemented the sea's bounty by subsistence farming or backyard farming. While agriculture subsistence and organic farming in particular, have experienced a resurgence, the

Department of Agriculture in conjunction with the Agricultural Society have been running the Agriculture Show for over 48 years.

The show is a widely anticipated family event every year and provides farmers with an opportunity to sell their home-grown produce and display their livestock. In addition to the wide selection of local produce, authentic dishes and handmade crafts are available for sale; children can participate in the many kid-friendly activities such as games, pageants, horseback riding and the petting zoo.

Now in its 49th year, the Agricultural Show is a testament to the love the people of these islands have for the land. Held every Ash Wednesday, a public holiday, it is not to be missed! Go early to avoid the traffic.

Cayman Easter

Easter is a very festive time in Cayman: Caymanians celebrate the occasion by camping on beaches, many attend church services and there are Easter brunches at numerous hotels and restaurants. Rum Point is also a popular meeting point for groups with boats, and some families rent condos in Cayman Kai. For a more adventurous Easter break, plane charters are often arranged to destinations such as

Honduras, Costa Rica or Panama, leaving on the Thursday night and returning on the Monday.

Batabano

Cayman Carnival Batabano is usually held the week after Easter every year, and will be held on 29th April 2017. It is a major highlight on the Island's entertainment calendar. The festival's name is a salute to Cayman's turtling heritage: it is said the word batabano refers to the tracks left in the sand by sea turtles as they crawl onto the beach to nest.

Batabano is a four day event that includes a Carnival Ball, soca song competition, street parade, street dance, a beach fête and pulsating Soca music, dancing and pageantry. It celebrates the Caribbean's diverse African and religious roots, as well as the colourful costumes that reflect the Island's rich heritage. Thousands of Cayman's locals and visitors (many travelling to Cayman just for this event) flock to the streets. It should not be missed! For more information visit the Batabano website at www.caymancarnival.com.

Rundown The Play

This popular local show is named after a spicy Caymanian dish that combines lots of different ingredients. The format is a series of skits, music, stand-up comedy, monologues, dance and impersonations. It is a gentle satirical look at Caymanian life, politics and its people. For more information call (345) 949 5477 or visit www.artscayman.org.

Halloween in Cayman

Halloween is a very popular event; costumes are planned weeks in advance and parents stock up on sweets for the countless trick-or-treaters that come knocking. The festivities start just as the sun goes down (wear bug spray) and are wrapped up by about 8pm.

Very popular areas to trick-or-treat are Webster's Estates (off South Sound) and Snug Harbour but people also trick-or-treat in their neighbourhoods. Camana Bay also hosts a family Halloween Spooktacular on or before October 31st, where kids dress up and take their loot bags around the stores for coveted candy and homemade treats!

Pirates Week

Cayman's National Festival Pirates Week, will run from Thursday 9th November to Monday 13th November 2017 in Grand Cayman. The festivities in Cayman Brac will be held between November 3rd and 5th 2017 and in Little Cayman from November 17th to 19th. This year

Pirates Week will be celebrating its 40th year. It is the country's largest celebration drawing some 35,000 patrons.

Heritage Days, which used to be held in each district, will now be condensed into a one-day event on November 13th 2017 in the district of George Town. All the usual Pirates Week events will be held over a long weekend various street dances in George Town, a float parade and landing pageant, two firework shows, a steel pan competition, two swim meets and a kids' fun day on the Sunday.

Cayman Christmas

Christmas in Cayman is magical! There might not be snow, but we do put up real Christmas trees and fill our gardens with twinkling lights as the rounds of parties and good cheer begin.

Traditions include visiting Capt. Theo Bodden's magnificent garden, opposite Sunset House, which from early-December becomes a theatrical display of lights. The festive season ticks off with the Christmas breeze which starts to blow in November.

Camana Bay's annual tree lighting is a great family outing. Later on in the month is the Parade of Lights (where boats decked with lights parade in the Camana Bay harbour, while the National Choir and school choirs sing carols).

The Rotary's annual carol singing concert in early December is highly anticipated every year. Enjoy shopping at the craft market and keep a look out for an appearance from Father Christmas!

Date System

The Cayman Islands use the English date system: day/month/year. However, because of the influence of the US, some people write the date as month/day/year.

While Cayman businesses and government institutions normally use the English date system, business forms will usually indicate whether the date or month comes first. If you are dating a professional document, you may enquire how the date should be written if you are unsure. A good rule-of-thumb is to write out the month.

English Date System Examples: 21st, May 2017 or 21/05/17

US Date System Examples: May 21, 2017 or 05/21/17

Business & Banking Hours

Most banks in the Cayman Islands are open Monday-Thursday from 9am-4pm and Friday from 9am-4.30pm but some bank branches are also open on Saturdays between 9am-1pm.

By law, most businesses in Cayman close on Sunday. Places that do remain open include some pharmacies, gas stations, major restaurants, hotels (including their bars), Camana Bay's cinema and even the Mountain Dew Black Pearl Skate Park.

Emergency services in the Cayman Islands such as police stations, fire departments and the public hospital remain open seven days per week, 24-hours per day.

Greeting Customs

The greeting customs of the Islands are as follows: always say "Good morning," or "Good evening" on first meeting someone. If you are talking to a Caymanian, then we usually use the first name but preface it with a 'Miss' or a 'Mr'. 'Mrs' is rarely used.

The Cayman Islands or "CayMAN" as the locals say (and never the 'Caymans') is generally a welcoming place and the 'Caymankindness' found in the country is embodied by many, so be sure to engage with people you meet if you are a first time visitor.

Caymankind is a local's way of presenting themselves to the world: they are generally courteous, compassionate and caring. People here will usually greet you with a smile or say a warm hello or perhaps even say something to make your day brighter than it already was. That's Caymankindess!

Business
Establishing a Business

The Cayman Islands has a well-regulated and internationally respected, tax-neutral, offshore business environment that is both dynamic and responsive there are over 100,000 active registered companies here.

So, establishing a business in the Cayman Islands has never been easier! Enhancing this business friendly environment even further was the Government's move to tighten the country's copyright legislation in June 2016, which provided more protection on patents and the rights of persons and companies involved in creative pursuits film, art, music, digital media etc.

As diverse businesses from film and finance to tech development move to Cayman to take advantage of our Special Economic Zone, Cayman's improved legislation will provide even more confidence to international clients, heightening the profile of the jurisdiction.

As a sophisticated, leading financial centre, Cayman also benefits from a stable government and a well-developed Common Law system based on English law. With a proliferation of world class corporate and service companies, it is not surprising that leading corporations choose to operate in the country.

Read on to learn about how to set up a business in the Cayman Islands.

Legal Formalities

A business in the Cayman Islands can be run as a sole trader operation, a partnership or a limited company. It is also possible for a foreign company to register a branch in the Cayman Islands in order for the foreign company to operate locally.

A business in Cayman can be run as a *sole trader* operation, a *partnership* or a *company*. It is also possible for a foreign company to register a branch in the Cayman Islands in order for the foreign company to operate locally.

The main distinction is that sole traders and general partners have unlimited liability to third parties doing business with them, whereas the shareholders of a company typically have limited liability to third parties doing business with the company.

Sole Trader

Due to immigration requirements and the rules governing the grant of a T&B Licence, in practise, only a Caymanian will be able to operate a business as a sole trader if they are competing in the domestic market. A sole trader is able to start his/her business without any formalities by simply offering services or goods in return for payment.

The sole trader can employ people to work in the business, but is personally responsible for all the liabilities of the business (e.g. rent, T&B Licence fees, salaries and benefits of employees) and is also the person who receives all the profits.

The differences in, and suitability of, various types of business structure are highly technical and are best discussed with a qualified Cayman Islands attorney. Typically, small owner-operated businesses with few liabilities, might consider operating as a sole trader (often using a 'trading as' title such as Fred Smith (t.a. Fred's Fantastic Fences). There are few formalities for formation and few annual fees.

However, the sole trader is personally responsible for any debts the business incurs. Due to immigration requirements and the rules governing the grant of a T&B Licence, in practise, only a Caymanian will be able to operate a business as a sole trader if they are competing in the domestic market.

A sole trader is able to start his/her business without any formalities by simply offering services or goods in return for payment. The sole trader can employ people to work in the business, but is personally responsible for all the liabilities of the business (e.g. rent, T&B Licence fees, salaries and benefits of employees) and is also the person who receives all the profits.

As indicated above, however, a foreign national competing only in the international economy from a base within the Cayman Islands, will generally only be able to obtain a licence and operate in and from within the Cayman Islands if they first incorporate a suitable Cayman Islands company and obtain suitable licensing for that entity. There will be no requirement for such an entity to have any Caymanian participation.

Partnerships

One form of partnership is where all the partners are "general" partners and participate in the management of the business. In this structure, the only restrictions on sharing profits and withdrawing capital are those agreed between the partners. As well as general partnerships, the Partnership Law sets out the rules for "ordinary" limited partnerships. However, limited partners must not participate in the management of the business and a limited partner's right to share in the profits or withdraw capital is restricted

Where two or more people want to go into business together but wish to avoid all the formalities and expense of a company, they would use a partnership structure. Professional advisors, such as lawyers and accountants, have traditionally used a partnership structure for their business. A partnership has less legislative governance than a company and can be more flexible in its treatments of the partners' responsibility for liabilities and share of profits. Partners are also personally liable for any debts the business incurs.

One form of partnerships is where all the partners are "general" partners and participate in the management of the business. In this structure, the only restrictions on sharing profits and withdrawing capital are those agreed between the partners.

As well as general partnerships, the Partnership Law sets out the rules for "ordinary" limited partnerships. However, limited partners must not participate in the management of the business and a limited partner's right to share in the profits or withdraw capital is restricted.

The exempted limited partnership is another form of partnership which is specially designed to provide more flexibility to suit the needs of the financial industry in Cayman. The Cayman Islands Exempted Limited Partnership Lawwas enacted on July 2, 2014.

It introduces changes intended to simplify, clarify and add flexibility to the establishment and ongoing operation of Cayman exempted limited partnerships. In all cases, you are advised to contact a specialist to determine the partnership arrangement most suitable for your needs

Companies & LLC

Foreign businesses that do not wish to establish a Cayman Islands subsidiary, do have the option of registering a branch operation in Cayman. The process to register a branch with the Cayman Registrar of Companies is straightforward and the branch, once registered, is required to maintain a local registered agent and pay annual fees to the Cayman Islands Government to maintain its registration

A company will be used where the owners and operators of the business want to have limited liability for the debts of the business. Companies are very commonly used for all sorts of businesses, from one-person operations to multi-million dollar, multinational businesses. There are more formalities and fees associated with forming and operating a company, than with a partnership or sole trader business, but many people feel the limited liability a company affords is worth the extra effort and cost.

Companies & LLCForeign businesses that do not wish to establish a Cayman Islands subsidiary, do have the option of registering a branch operation in Cayman. The process to register a branch with the Cayman Registrar of Companies is straightforward and the branch, once registered, is required to maintain a local registered agent and pay annual fees to the Cayman Islands Government to maintain its registration.

If your aim is to operate a business on-Island, then depending on the nature of the 'on-island' business to be conducted some other form of local licensing will be needed. More detail on the Local Licences procedure is given later in this section.

For a business wholly or at least 60% beneficially owned and controlled by one or more Caymanians, the acquisition of a Trade and Business (T&B) Licence is required. Where beneficial ownership and control is less than 60% by Caymanians, a Local Companies Control Law Licence ("LCCL") may be required. The grant of an LCCL is a matter of discretion for the Trade & Business Licensing Board which will carefully consider, amongst other things, the benefit such business will bring to the Islands, the extent to which Caymanian participation has been sought (which will ordinarily include a requirement for public advertising) and whether the proposed business will compete with local Caymanian owned businesses.

Businesses wishing to set up a physical presence in the Cayman Islands, whose activities are carried on mainly outside the Islands, are in most cases exempted from the Local Companies Control Law (LCCL). Therefore, although they would require a T&B Licence to set up their local office and secure work permits for any expatriate employees (as discussed further in the Immigration chapter), they would not require an LCCL, or 60% ownership by a Caymanian Status holder.

It should be noted that banks, trust companies, company management firms and a number of other businesses are exempted from requiring both a T&B Licence and LCCL, though they would need to secure any requisite licensing with the Cayman Islands Monetary Authority (CIMA). A different regulatory regime is available for businesses in certain approved categories seeking to set up within Cayman's Special Economic Zone.

Trade & Business Licensing

In order for an individual, partnership or company to conduct business in or from the Cayman Islands, an application must be made to the

Trade and Business Licensing Board for the grant of a T&B Licence (subject to limited exceptions).

Trade and Business Licensing is necessary if a company wants to conduct business in Cayman. If the company does not have at least 60% Caymanian ownership and control, it will also require an LCCL from the Trade and Business Licensing Board (unless it is otherwise exempted from such requirement).

The T&B Licence fee is payable every year and the application for renewal must be made at least 28 days before the anniversary of the grant of the T&B licence. It is an offence to operate a business without a valid T&B Licence or an alternative licence (unless exempted).

Incorporation/ Registration

If you wish to establish a business in the Cayman Islands, you are required to engage a local licensed service provider to incorporate your company.

The incorporation and registration of a businesses is a seamless process conducted by a licensed local corporate service provider. Most firms also provide these services: registered office, nominee shareholders, directors and other officers and management of the company on the instruction of the beneficial owner(s).

Online registration is also now available and accessible through local licensed service providers.

This is secure access and <u>not</u> available to the public. Read on to see a list of top firms under Corporate Services. The Registrar of Companies may be contacted on (Tel: (345) 946 7922), Ground Floor, Government Administration Building, 133 Elgin Avenue, George Town.

Learn about the application process below.

Application Process

The **application process** to register your company is straight forward and your local licensed service provider will:

1. Contact the Registrar of Companies and ask if the company name you want is available
2. Prepare the following documents (and other documents may be required based on the type of company you are incorporating):
Memorandum of Association;
Articles of Association;
A cover letter providing details of the proposed business;

The fees for incorporation vary depending on the type of company and share capital. For a typical local company with a share capital of less than CI$42,000, the fee is CI$300 and for an exempt company the minimum fee would be CI$600. Your local service provider will have their own fee list. The company is deemed incorporated on the day the incorporation documents and fees are submitted to the Registrar.

The processing time for return of the proof of incorporation (namely the **certificate of incorporation**, Registrar stamped and certified Memorandum and Articles of Association) is approximately three to four business days, unless submitted on an express basis (for an additional fee of CI$400) in which case, the proof of incorporation will be returned the following business day.

The Companies Registry will require some categories of companies, such as exempt companies, to have a local licensed service provider maintain the company's registered office.

Company Registry Fees

The registration and annual fees for any company are dependent on the size of the authorised share capital. Also worth noting is that licence fees are due annually in January of each year, but the Companies Registry is under no obligation to notify the company that the fees are due.

If these fees are not paid by the 31 March (of each year), they begin to accrue penalties up to *100% of the fee!* Every company is responsible for paying these annual fees and if you do not pay them the company will usually be struck off the register of Cayman Islands incorporated companies. If the company had any assets at the time it was struck off, those assets will become the property of the Government of the Cayman Islands.

If you were ignorant of the fact that annual fees were due, your company could be struck off without your knowledge. This is one of the benefits of using a local licensed service provider, as they will process the annual paperwork and remind you of the amount and timing of annual fees. Their fees are a lot less than the fees you would pay to an attorney to make the necessary application to the Cayman Court for the company to be re-instated to the registry!

Corporate Services

There are many professionals and business who can assist with the process of incorporating a business in the Cayman Islands. These local licensed corporate service providers usually charge a fee of between US$700–US$1,250, excluding government filing fees, for their services.

The other services they offer include: the provision of a registered office; maintenance of statutory registers; handling of annual returns; drafting resolutions and minutes; providing certified documents;

getting documents apostilled and notarised; updating the register of officers, shareholders and directors; maintaining the minute book; assisting with corporate restructuring; revisions to the memo and arts, and some also provide director services.

Opening Business Accounts

To create a bank account for a company incorporated in Cayman, the bank or trust company will need the following information:

- ✓ Full incorporation paperwork
- ✓ Bank references from a current bank
- ✓ A letter giving an overview of the business and reason for needing the account
- ✓ Certificate of Incorporation, certified by a Notary Public
- ✓ Articles and Memorandum of Association, certified by a Notary Public
- ✓ Register of Members, Officers and Directors certified by the registered office or a Notary Public
- ✓ The minutes of the directors' first meeting also certified by the registered office

- ✓ The identity of each ultimate beneficial owner, director and signatory; this must be supported by a certified copy of their passports and proof of residential address
- ✓ If the business is conducted within the Cayman Islands, a copy of the current Trade and Business Licence
- ✓ Professional reference from an accounting or law firm and a professional reference from a bank that indicates a good relationship of over three years
- ✓ Nature and dollar volume of anticipated transactions including source of funding of initial and subsequent deposits. This can be provided from a copy of the Business Plan if the company is new or latest Financial Statements if the company is already operating
- ✓ Bank paperwork duly filled out
- ✓ All directors, members and signatories to supply all information needed for a personal bank account

If you have been personally interviewed at the bank, then you don't need a certification of identification. If there are more than a nominal number of shareholders, the bank requires identification and references for the principal shareholders who own 10% or more of the shareholding, directors and officers responsible for the operation of the account.

Companies incorporated in other countries require notarised documents to verify the bona fides of the company. The minimum opening deposit is CI$2,500 or currency equivalent.

Business Services

In this section the Cayman Resident provides the Cayman Islands' most comprehensive guide to all the business services in the country from detailed information about each service to contact details, including all the locations of the top companies, legal and accounting firms and corporate service providers. We also show you how to keep your business secure and protected from fraud.

The companies we list will provide support while you set up a business in the Cayman Islands or can help with the day-to-day needs of an established business.

From advertising to other necessary business services such as having a company print your signs... to cleaning up the office after a long day, we've tried to list all the top companies in the Cayman Islands that will greatly assist you in running your business effectively and efficiently.

You will also find useful tips on how to keep your business secure plus a free hotline to call if you wish to report business fraud anonymously.

Accounting & Auditing Firms

The Cayman Islands is one of the top financial centres in the world, therefore you will find some of the top international accounting firms on Grand Cayman. Most are full service firms.

Accounting firms in the Cayman Islands provide a broad range of advisory, administrative, auditing and consulting services to their local and international clientele, so it is not surprising that the country is a well regulated business environment.

Below is a list of the top accounting firms and associations operating in the Cayman Islands.

BDO

BDO is one of the world's leading accountancy networks, providing a range of tax, audit, advisory and outsourcing services
Tel: +1 345 943 8800Email: mail@bdo.kywww.bdo.ky

. **EisnerAmper Cayman Ltd**.

A leading firm of accountants and business advisers who audit hedge funds, captive insurance companies and trusts companies.
Tel: +1 345 945 5889Email: bleung@eisneramper.kywww.eisneramper.ky

Baker Tilly (Cayman) Ltd.

Baker Tilly (Cayman) Ltd. is a leading firm of Chartered Accountants and Business Advisors in the Cayman Islands.

Tel: +1 345 946 7853 Email: info@bakertillycayman.com www.bakertillycayman.com

Cayman Islands Institute of Professional Accountants (CIIPA)

Tel: +1 345 749 3360 Email: admin@ciipa.ky www.cispa.ky

KPMG

KPMG provides audit, tax and advisory services and industry insight.

Tel: +1 345 949 4800 Email: kpmg@kpmg.ky www.kpmg.ky

Deloitte

One of Cayman's largest professional Service firms offering accounting, consultancy, financial, tax and risk advisory

Tel: +1 345 949 7500

Attorneys & Law Firms in Cayman

Cayman's top legal firms are internationally known, solution driven and client focused. These global players are able to attract top talent from London to Hong Kong, even from London's magic circle firms...

Most of Cayman's top firms specialise in corporate and international finance law, focusing on investment funds, capital markets and structured finance. Cayman law firms are also internationally renowned for advising top asset managers and institutional investors from around the world, as well being involved in high level international insolvency and restructuring deals. It is not surprising that the legal industry on Island continues to experience growth.

Additionally, criminal and corporate litigation services are usually offered by all the major firms on Island. The Cayman Islands Law is based on English common law with local statutes. English statutes have been extended to the Cayman Islands and the Islands have a stable legal and judicial system that is being constantly developed to meet the demands of a growing country.

Corporate Service Providers

Here we list companies that supply corporate services ranging from enterprise-wide needed support to simply assisting with necessary paperwork.

These Cayman companies can supply corporate services ranging from the formation of local or foreign companies or partnerships. They can also provide registered office facilities and other services like the payment of fees and the preparation and filing of annual returns.

Other services may include the liquidation or cessation of businesses and/or partnerships.

Business Security

Although Cayman has one of the lowest crime rates in the region, the Royal Cayman Islands Police (RCIP) is taking a proactive approach to mitigate any criminal activity within the business community.

Business security is a top priority for business owners in the Cayman Islands. The Royal Cayman Islands Police (RCIP) run a Business Watch programme along the George Town waterfront that allows business owners to report any suspicious behavior directly to PC Jonathan Kern: (Email jonathan.kern@rcips.ky or Tel: +1 (345) 649 4222).

Additionally, reports can be made anonymously via the RCIP call centre in Miami Tel: 1-800-TIPS. By reporting even the smallest annoyance, the police can recognise if a trend is occurring in your area and jump on the problem before anything bigger occurs. If you witness a crime or are being threatened at your business, please contact 911 directly. The RCIP plans to launch the Business Watch programme in other areas in the near future.

If you need to improve the security at your business, here are some companies that provide services from 24- hour security monitoring to installing alarm systems:

The Security Centre Limited
Complete security and automation solutions for homes and businesses and to suit every budget.
Tel: +1 345 949 004 Email: info@security.ky www.security.ky

Islands Electronics Security & Monitoring Ltd.
A security monitoring and supply company that has been in business in the Cayman Islands since 1986.
Tel: +1 345 949 8255

Notary Public/Justice of the Peace

There are times when you will need documents to be certified as true and correct copies for work permit applications, opening a bank account, renewing your passport, buying a house etc. In these instances local Notary Public or Justice of the Peace services are available either through law firms or from independent operators.

Justices usually do not charge but they are somewhat limited in the documents they can certify. It is always a good idea to have a passport or driver's licence handy when you need their services.

Visit www.judicial.ky to find a list of all Notaries and Justices that are in good standing. You will be expected to pay the Notary Public in the region of CI$25 per stamp, though some charge less if it is just a simple matter of notarising the same signature on various documents. Some charge a call-out fee if you want them to visit you to notarise documents.

Below are a few Notaries Public and Justices of the Peace in the Cayman Islands that you can call:

Baysyde Biz

They provide secretarial and notary public services in regular business hours or outside of business hours in the event of an emergency. Tel: +1 345 917 5756Email: baysydebiz@gmail.com

Legal Chambers Cayman Ltd

Noel Webb - Tel: +1 (345) 926 8080

Tel: +1 345 936 5222

Email: info@legalchamberscayman.comwww.legalchamberscayman.com

Anti-Business Fraud Hotline

The implementation of Cayman's landmark Anti-Fraud Policy is underway and in 2017, the Cayman Islands Government established a whistle-blower hotline in order for civil servants and members of the public to report government fraud or breaches in ethics anonymously. The number for the toll-free hotline is Tel: 1 (800) 534 1111. All calls to this hotline will be monitored and answered overseas by a KPMG trained operator. Callers can expect to receive a tracking number, which can then be used as a reference if they need to make a follow-up call.

Persons who wish to make a report by email must use fraud@kpmg.co.za and are encouraged to visit the Anti-Fraud Policy website at www.fraud.gov.ky if they require more information. All claims of fraud or allegations will be investigated by Cayman's Internal Audit Service.

Advertising Agencies & Public Relations Firms

Do you need help promoting your brand? Are you eager to stand out from the crowd? It is important that you choose the right advertising agency!

Luckily, the Cayman Islands has a great selection of creative agencies providing exceptional advertising, marketing, branding and public relations services, that can provide you with the right tools to promote your business on Island.

Before asking for a pitch from several agencies, first look through their websites to see if you like the look of their previous work, read the testimonials of previous clients, and finally ask each agency how they think they will be able to help you.

From branding and running advertising campaigns to producing print Ads and videos, these Cayman agencies are just a phone call away...

Aguru Limited

Aguru is a new marketing agency delivering solutions for clients primarily across the Caribbean and also international locations.

Tel: +1 (345) 949 7057

BB&P

BB&P work to transform your business prospects and give you a competitive advantage with a reasonably-priced branding system.

Tel: +1 (345) 949 2933

FSH Design

Providing Marketing, Strategic Planning, Advertising and Public Relations.

Tel: +1 (345) 947 8755

Fountainhead

Fountainhead is a specialist marketing and business development

agency providing access to both international and domestic markets.
Tel: +1 345 945 8188

MC2

Providing Graphic Design, Marketing and Advertising solutions for your business.
Tel: +1 (345) 946 1220

Commercial Real Estate

In this section we advise on finding commercial properties in Grand Cayman, give an overview of renting office or retail space, typical leasing costs and give insider tips on new developments

Commercial Office Space

The Cayman Islands maintains the largest office market of all the offshore financial centres in the Caribbean. From newly appointed Class A new builds in Camana Bay to elegant old offices in George Town overlooking the harbour, Cayman has a wide range commercial properties for rent and sale

Finding a commercial property on Grand Cayman is not a challenge, whether you are looking to buy an entire building or lease a small office space. You just have to know what you are looking for. Before you commit to a property, we recommend that you read about the latest happenings in the world of commercial real estate on Grand Cayman and of course contact a local realtor who specialises in commercial properties.

The Grand Cayman commercial office space rental market is one of the strongest in the Caribbean region with high demand for all classes of office space traditionally in the region of 75,000 sq ft to 125,000 sq ft per annum, primarily from the offshore financial sector. In recent years, however, the absorption rate has been at the lower end of this range although this has been rising during 2016.

The market comprises close to 3.5 million square feet of office space in all classes, which breaks down to roughly 1.25 million square feet of Class A space, 2 million square feet of Class B space and the remainder as Class C.

Average vacancy rates vary by class and location from as low as 2-3% for Class A to A+ space, 5-10% for Class B+ to A- and around 15%-20% for Class B and C space. Within these averages, there is a wide variety of vacancies, with some Class B properties in central George Town with vacancies of between 40% to 75%. This has been largely due to the exodus of top quality, larger corporate tenants from the typically older buildings in George Town Centre to the master-planned community of Camana Bay or edge of town development corridor of Elgin Avenue.

Class A to A+ space is predominantly now found in development type locations such as Camana Bay and Cricket Square on Elgin Avenue. These consist of hurricane rated buildings, typically at elevations well above the Hurricane Ivan flood plain of 8', with ample parking and high quality on-site amenities including restaurants, conference facilities and gyms.

Rental rates range on a triple net basis from US$42 to US$52 psf pa in the class A to A+ market sector with the highest rents in Camana Bay to US$30 to US$40 per sq.ft. in the Class B+ to A- market sector, falling to US$20 to US$28 psf pa in the Class B market. They charges range from between US$15 to US$18 psf pa in developments such as Cricket Square and Camana Bay where infrastructure costs are higher, to between US$11 to US$14 per sq ft per annum in standalone office buildings in other locations.

More recently, as gross rent rates in developments such as Camana Bay and Cricket Square have risen to between US$65 US$72 per sq ft per annum and those in central George Town have fallen to not much more than half this amount, the trend has reversed and increasing numbers of tenants are now choosing office space located in buildings within George Town centre once again.

This is especially the case with law firms who need court access and small to medium sized firms in the offshore finance industry. As such, the current prognosis for George Town looks positive, especially with bearing in mind the potential for the new cruise ship dock that may bring new restaurants and other amenities back into the capital.

Cannon Place

51 units available for rent, Serviced Office Suites, Board Rooms and Training Rooms. Serviced Office Suites fitted out to high standards. Tel: +1 345 944 3517Email: scott.clare@rpmcayman.comwww.cannonplace.ky

Setting Up an Office

In this section we provide information on setting up an office and fitting it out with everything from office furniture, networking solutions to telephone and internet service, as well as options for professional training.

The length of time required for setting up an office depends on the finished condition of the space and how closely this meets your requirements. The simplest of offices can be set up in as little as 4 to 8 weeks, however, most offices do not come together this quickly.

By the time a design has been finalised, interior finishes have been chosen, furniture ordered, IT systems specified and work permits and licences granted, you should expect about four to six months to have passed. It should also be noted that tenants may be required to submit fit-out plans to the Planning Department for building code approval in advance.

Office Space Planning & Design

The Cayman Islands has architectural firms with qualified interior architects and designers specializing in corporate interiors, many with extensive international experience. In the progressive climate of today's global business world, creating a successful and enduring corporate workplace goes well beyond merely designing beautiful spaces.

It is important to start the design on a comprehensive brief defining functional and aesthetic requirements which can include setting goals for the promotion of your team's wellbeing, accounting for technological advancements in your industry or articulating your company's core values as they may apply to a physical space.

Involving your designer prior to selecting a new office space can be very beneficial as they may assist in evaluating available spaces for your company's needs prior to agreement to lease or purchase. This analysis may involve a 'test fit' of the space to ensure it will meet either short and/or long term requirements, check lease area measurements and evaluate base building mechanical, electrical and communications infrastructure.

With a current trend towards 'open plan' offices requiring less space per employee, creating a successful 'open' plan requires skillful space planning. Providing areas of acoustic and visual isolation responsive to your unique organizational needs will help to limit unwanted disruptions and loss of focus whilst still maintaining the goal of an open office environment of shared natural light, flexibility and connectivity of your employees.

Many people have a great deal of difficulty in visualizing a spatial layout from two dimensional plan drawings. When looking at proposed designs with your design team, 3D representations can be a great help in visualising your new workplace in the early phases of the design process. These visual aids can be valuable in clarifying the design intent before progressing with detailed documents that are required for construction and obtaining required statutory approvals. All fitout works in Cayman are required to meet our local building code requirements, plans and specifications must be submitted to the Central Planning Authority to obtain a building permit prior to construction.

Many architectural firms also have experience in working with international rating authorities such as LEED, Green Star, BREEAM, WELL Building Standard and other globally recognized rating systems that promote more sustainable, energy-efficient and healthy fit-outs. These standards can benchmark your organisation's commitment to creating a better workplace against internationally recognized industry standards.

Costs to Prepare Office Space

The cost of preparing an office depends on a number of factors, including the existing condition of the space and the quality of the final product. Well-fitted existing office space in need of reconfiguration, with partitioned walls and internal offices, a suspended ceiling, fluorescent lighting, air conditioning and power grid already in place, can be prepared for as little as US$50 per sq ft.

Finding such space is limited, though, so it is more typical to find a new space with only perimeter walls, one to two hour fire rating separation walls and an air conditioning unit with an electrical panel sufficient for the tenants' requirements. For space like this, you will likely spend US$120-US$200 per sq ft to prepare it to a reasonably high quality fit-out. Some landlords will offer a standard fit-out package, or a fit-out allowance, in the region of US$15-US$30 per sq ft depending on the location

Fitting Out Your Office

Have you purchased a new commercial building or moved your business to a new office space? Sometimes it can feel as if you are starting all over again, and we agree that fitting out a new space can feel overwhelming!

But fitting out your office in the Cayman Islands is a painless process because we make it easy! Cayman Resident provides you with all the well-known architectural firms on Island that have qualified interior designers who specialise in the design of commercial properties plus experienced contractors.

These professionals can take a new or existing office and create a space to suit the requirements of your business.

Office Furniture

Whether you are furnishing your new office or updating outdated office furniture in an existing office, there are only a couple of companies in Cayman that are able to help with the professional installation of office furniture. These companies also sell a wide range of office furniture.

Companies that sell office furniture also have staff on-hand that will help you choose the right office furniture and help layout your office space to ensure employees remain comfortable and efficient. Some of these companies will allow you to test-out office furniture such as special swivel chairs, for a short period, before committing to a purchase.

The companies below can help.

Kirk Office

Kirk Office are an authorised retailer of Apple, HP and Lenovo and they have the latest computers, tablets and accessories on display.

Tel: (345) 623 5475 Email: info@kirk.ky www.kirkoffice.ky

Office Supply

Offers a wide selection of office products, computers, electronic accessories and comprehensive IT support.
Tel: +1 345 946 1200 Email: info@officesupply.ky www.officesupply.ky

Telephone & Internet

Among other things, you will need to find, choose and install a telephone system, internet access and telephone service from a local carrier. For various providers and the plans they offer, along with their contact details see the Telecommunications & Internet page.

Choosing a telephone and internet carrier can be challenging, as there are different delivery methods (wired, wireless), rates and interconnection choices. The right combination of these choices can make quite a difference to your office experience and your monthly service bills. You may choose to use your own telephone system and direct your outgoing calls through a carrier with the lowest costs and the best line quality. Most of the local carriers now offer low cost Voice Over IP (VoIP) calling, which allows for very low rates for international dialing.

Telecommunication standards differ from those in North America, where the T1 line type is the standard for delivering high density call traffic. Here in Cayman the E1 (European standard) line type is the connection of choice. It has the advantage of supporting more simultaneous calls over the same dedicated line. For internet, traditional data services such as ADSL and data circuits are available. A service called MPLS is also becoming increasingly popular, and this allows for cost effective high bandwidth connections to overseas offices, which is a flexible alternative to static international data circuits. Carriers can also offer diversity and redundancy for voice/data links to the Islands.

Grand Cayman is serviced by two underwater fibre links: MAYA1 which connects most of the western Caribbean nations, before returning to the US and Cayman Jamaica Fibre System (CJFS) that takes an alternative route via the eastern Caribbean back to the US. En-route to Jamaica, the CJFS fibre also transitions Cayman Brac. Albeit with limited capacity, voice and data services can also be provided via satellite so that your office can communicate should your chosen carrier be unable to provide service during or after a hurricane.

Cell phone service providers provide data for Blackberries and other smart phones. Typically, sending and receiving messages and emails is relatively inexpensive, but you should check the cross-carrier rates and sign-up for a data plan that best suits your needs. International cell phone roaming, like anywhere in the world, can be very expensive unless your provider has regional rates across the Caribbean.

Transmission speeds are on par with US providers, with fast data mobile services, such as 4G (Flow, formerly LIME and Digicel) technologies that are starting to emerge. Additionally, number portability has now been available for about 2 years.

With the general reduction in internet costs, many businesses are now providing free Wi-Fi. Camana Bay, for example, has free internet access on the entire property, as do most of the local hotels.

Networks

Electrical and wiring standards generally follow those of North America, so installing and configuring standard telephone and computer equipment shouldn't present any problems. 120AV is the power standard, 60 cycle with a standard plug style (dual pin with ground).

Internationally known names such as HP, CISCO, Checkpoint and Mitel are all represented on Cayman and you will find that local vendors can meet all of your VoIP, networking, storage (NAS and SAN), data security and disaster recovery needs.

Manufacturers' warranties on failed hardware are honoured for equipment purchased on-Island from authorised dealers. Comprehensive Disaster Recovery (DR) services are now available within the Cayman Islands, with the option to vault data on short notice within protected hurricane resistant data centres.

Professional Training

There are numerous training centres on Island, much of which specifically caters to the financial services industry.

However, the range of other training possibilities are varied and encompasses medicine, law, veterinary, accounting, banking, *human resource management* and education, to name just a few, and as of September 2012, nursing.

There are also vocational training courses for occupational health and safety certificates relevant to the construction industry, as well as *nanny certifications*, CPR courses and numerous computer and language courses.

Colleges and other tertiary educational centres in Cayman also offer short certification courses, visit this page for more. For Training Centres that can help get you or your staff on track see the list below.

Community Vocational Training Centre

Courses are open to students aged 17+ and there are no entry requirements. Students work towards a professional licence or to meet local industry standards to become an electrician, plumber, welder or a/c technician. Courses are held in the evenings from 6pm-9pm. Call Allan Moore on (345) 917 7320.

Chamber of Commerce Professional Development & Training Centre

A range of one or two full-day courses are offered to assist businesses develop their employees. Seminars and workshops are held in the areas of customer service and business essentials, business basics, finance, supervision and management. For more info call (345) 949 8090 or check out the courses online at www.caymanchamber.ky/training.

Innovative Management & Professional Training (IMPT)

They offer two accounting programmes: the ACCA Qualification and the Foundations in Accountancy, as well as the ICSA certificate in Offshore Finance and Administration, the Certificate in Offshore Banking Practice (from the Chartered Banker) and Certifications in Management from the Institute of Leadership and Management (ILM). They also offer computer training courses and various business skills training courses. Unit 201, Alissta Towers, 85 North Sound Road, George Town, Tel: (345) 943 4678.

Passport2Success

In order to equip high school graduates in the Cayman Islands with the required skills to perform effectively in today's work place, the Ministry of Education, Employment and Gender Affairs, along with the support of major employers, have developed a workplace-readiness skills programme that focuses on developing skills through training seminars, therapeutic intervention, community service and work experience. Passport2Success is a full-time programme that lasts for 12 weeks, five days a week from 9am-4pm. The programme has been increasing the skills of unemployed Caymanians since April 2010. To apply for a place on the course, contact the National Workforce Development Agency on (345) 945 3114.

Risk Consultancy Services Ltd.

(RCS) Trains individuals/companies on the 30-hour OSA (Occupational Safety & Health) training programme. They offer training in rigging and lifting procedures for crane operations, fall protection training, scaffold building, forklift operator training, hazardous material handling, fire warden training and PHTLS training (pre-hospital trauma life support). Online training is available. Call Julius Jacky on (345) 326 1007 or email: Julius.jacky@rcs.ky for more information.

Education

For being such a small island, Cayman has a wide variety of excellent public and private schools from preschool all the way to university level. There are also a handful of adult classes available in case you are looking to start a new hobby or meet new people.

Schools & Education in Cayman

For the 2015-16 school calendar year, there were 2,456 students enrolled in government primary schools, 2,252 students enrolled in government secondary schools and 109 students enrolled in the Lighthouse School, the country's school for special needs.

There were 4,998 students in private schools (1,785 under the age of 4 years 9 months in preschools, 1,804 in primary schools and 1,409 in secondary schools). In Cayman, it is compulsory for all children from the age of four years and nine months to age 17 to attend school or be home-schooled.

How The Grade System Works

Grade/Year	British	American
Kindergarten (UK) Pre-K (US)	age 4 turning 5 (during that year)	age 5 turning 6
1	age 5 turning 6	age 6 turning 7
2	age 6 turning 7	age 7 turning 8
3	age 7 turning 8	age 8 turning 9
4	age 8 turning 9	age 9 turning 10
5	age 9 turning 10	age 10 turning 11
6	age 10 turning 11	age 11 turning 12
7	age 11 turning 12	age 12 turning 13
8	age 12 turning 13	age 13 turning 14
9	age 13 turning 14	age 14 turning 15
10	age 14 turning 15	age 15 turning 16
11	age 15 turning 16	age 16 turning 17
12/Lower 6th	age 16 turning 17	age 17 turning 18
13/Upper 6th	age 17 turning 18	

In the Cayman Islands compulsory education must start by 4yrs 9mths.

Caymanian Children

Caymanian students have the option to go to a government school (it is decided by catchment area) or a private school. All three government high schools end at Year 11 (age 16), but the government mandates that education is compulsory to Year 12 (age 17).

Many children then either move to a private high school in Cayman or to boarding school in Canada, the US or the UK. There is a huge culture in Cayman of children going away to boarding school. If they stay in Cayman, they can do a two-year A Level course (the UK system), and depending on the child's exam results, the parents can apply for all or part of the school fees to be paid for by the Ministry of Education.

Alternatively, they can go to the Cayman Islands Further Education Centre (CIFEC) and take a BTEC vocational course or, depending on their GCSE results and age (must be 17+), apply to attend the University College of the Cayman Islands (UCCI) and take an Associates degree.

Expat Children

It is the Cayman Islands government's stance that expatriates employed in the private sector who qualify to have their dependants on-Island with them (i.e. earn over CI$3,500 per month and have two dependants on their permit), should educate their children in private schools.

If the government employs the expatriate, then the employee has the option of sending their children to a government school if there is space.

If you are an expatriate on a work permit, the process is as follows: 1) apply to your chosen school; 2) get confirmation from the school by letter that your child has been accepted "pending Immigration approval"; 3) take this letter to Immigration along with your work permit application; 4) take a copy of the letter verifying that your child has been added as a dependant to your work permit to the school prior to attendance.

Reserving a place

Many private schools in Grand Cayman are in the enviable position of having long waiting lists for places in every year, particularly in kindergarten and Year 1.

As early as possible, and definitely before your child's first birthday, place their name on the list of your two preferred primary schools, and at birth for your preferred preschool. Siblings, children of alumni and members of the affiliated church (if it is a faith-based school) are usually given priority, so even if your child is on a waiting list, enrolment is not guaranteed. Do not overlook enrolling your subsequent children. The school will require a copy of your child's birth certificate (which they will photocopy and return to you), a passport sized photograph of your child and a completed application form. Many also require a deposit.

Enrolment Age & Requirements

For preschool, your child can usually start at age two or sometimes as young as 18 months. For primary school, the starting age depends on whether you will be educating your child through the British school system (Cayman Prep and High School (CPHS), St. Ignatius and government schools) or the American school system (Cayman International School, First Baptist School, Grace Christian Academy and Triple C).

In the British system, your child can enter Kindergarten if they are four by September, while in the American system, your child must be five by September. Please be aware that many of the private schools now have Pre-K years (e.g. St. Ignatius Catholic School and Cayman International School) which means that their students can start at 2 or 3 years old and will automatically move up to Kindergarten, leaving less space for incoming students. If you intend to send your child to one of the major private primary schools, make sure to secure and accept their place in kindergarten or you will find it very difficult to get them into the school in Grade 1.

Most private schools in Cayman will only test your child for placement if they are entering after Kindergarten (or Pre-K4). If your child is transferring from another school, they will likely need official school records from the previous school(s), if transferring at the high school level. An up-to-date medical record, that includes vaccination details, is also required.

Health Screenings

All students entering government or private schools in the Cayman Islands for the first time are required to have a health screening. The Education Department mandates that these screenings must be completed before the new school year begins in September. The screening includes a growth and development assessment, screening for vision and hearing, a dental assessment, the administration of necessary immunizations and obtaining a student's personal medical history. Public Health Department staff will conduct the screenings which are free to all students.

For those entering schools in West Bay and the Eastern districts, health screenings usually take place between the 1st and 30th of June. For all other students, health screenings will take place at John Gray High School Medical Centre (Nurse's Office) from 5th July to 18th August 2017.

Appointments can be made at the school the child will be attending. Parents and guardians need to accompany their children to the health screening and they should also bring the child's immunization record. Vaccines will be offered to children whose immunizations are not up-to-date. Parents may have their child's health screenings done by a private doctor, as long as that doctor completes the school health screening forms provided by the Public Health Department. The completed forms should be handed in at the John Gray High School Medical Centre (Nurse's Office) between 5 July and 18 August 2017, from 8.30am and 4.30pm.

In Cayman Brac and Little Cayman, appointments for school entry screenings can be made by contacting Public Health Nurse Paula Moore-Simpson at Faith Hospital on (345) 948 2243/244 7643. Detailed information sheets for parents and guardians are available at the schools. For more information, please contact Nurse Carvell Bailey on (345) 244 2734 and (345) 244 2648. If you have a query you can email the School Health Coordinator, Carvell Bailey, on carvell.bailey@hsa.ky.

School Uniforms

Almost all preschools do not have a school uniform policy but they encourage parents to bring children in clothes that they can easily play in and shoes that they can take on and off themselves. They will also require that your child brings a backpack to school with a change of clothes in it.

All primary and high schools, whether government or private have specified school uniforms and you are advised to organise them early or your child's size may well get sold out. Most of the schools sell their own or will let you know where to buy them. They also have a very specific shoe policy make sure to ask! Usually shoes must be black and have no special features on them. Black sneakers cannot be substituted for formal black school shoes. Many of the private schools also now, very wisely, have a hat policy. No hat, no play!

School Fees & Scholarships

School fees quoted on this page are for the 2017/18 calendar year and are subject to change.

Caymanian students do not pay school fees to attend government schools. All non-Caymanian students attending one of the public schools pay CI$750 per year for primary school, CI$900 per year for middle school and CI$1,200 per year for high school. This is considerably less expensive than current private school fees.

The fees for private schools vary widely from school to school. The top preschools charge in the region of CI$850-$985 per month, but you can find many daycare centres and nurseries that charge only CI$600 per month (for keeping your children from 7am to 6pm). The top primary schools charge between CI$8,500-CI$17,870 per year and the top high schools charge between CI$9,800-CI$19,200 per year, but lower fees can be found at other schools. Some schools offer a sibling discount. Most private schools also prefer fees to be paid per term or annually.

All Caymanian students accepted at a private school to take A Levels or an Associates degree at UCCI, can apply for a scholarship to help pay for their school fees. If a student is accepted from a government school, they get the first year's fees paid in full (plus text books) and then either CI$7,000 or CI$5,000 paid for the second year (it is decided on a points system based on the student's GCSE results). They also must have higher passes in GCSE and/or CXC (Caribbean Examination Council) English Language and Mathematics to secure funding. Current

Caymanian students of either CPHS or St. Ignatius can apply for funding when they enter Year 12 (and 13). All students must obtain a minimum of 2 Cs and a D passes in their AS levels at the end of Year 12 in order to get the funding for the second year of 6th form. The application period for local scholarship funding is March 1st to April 30th. Late applications will not be considered. For more information please see the Scholarships section of www.education.gov.ky.

Switching Schools

Many Caymanian students leave the public school system and go to a private school for A Levels. At the same time many expat children leave the private schools in Cayman and leave for boarding schools in England, Canada and the USA. The three main years of entry into a private school in Cayman, or a boarding school overseas, are at the beginning of high school (Year 7), at beginning of Year 9 (a year before GCSE's start) or at the beginning of Year 12 (for the start of A Levels). Since many parents in Cayman send their children to boarding school we have been reliably told that equal numbers of children leave for the start of years 5, 6, 7, 8 and 9, the final push being the year before children start GCSE's. When these pupils leave, places in private schools in Cayman are freed up and the places are quickly snapped up by Caymanian students leaving the government high schools.

Places at Cayman's two private schools which do A Levels (CPHS and St. Ignatius) are few and highly sought after. On average, there are no more than 10 places available for the start of 6th form (Year 12) and each child is expected to get an A or a B grade in the GCSE subjects which they have chosen to do at A Level. More public school students can gain a place at either of these private schools if they are willing to enter in years 7, 8 or 9. In all instances, the child will be interviewed and expected to meet the school's evaluation criteria.

If you do want to enter your child into either of these private schools, you must apply no later than January of the year in which your child wishes to start. By the start of the Easter term they will have effectively closed their lists to new applicants.

Quite a few students also switch between the private schools, but before a switch can take place, and in addition to the normal paperwork (assessments etc.), there is a transfer form, designed and managed by the Private Schools Association (PSA), that must be completed by the current school and forwarded to the new school. As well as a standard report on the child's performance and behaviour, this form clearly states whether financial commitments have been met. It is an essential component of the acceptance process for students transferring within the private school system.

Public Education

Students enrolling in government primary and high schools must register with the Department of Education Services, 130 Thomas Russell Way, George Town, Grand Cayman or the Cayman Brac Teacher's Centre, between mid-May and mid-July.

Government Primary Schools

Seven of Grand Cayman's eight government primary schools now have a Kindergarten/Reception year; leaving Red Bay Primary School, as the only government primary school that starts students in Grade 1, at the age of five (must be five by August 31st of the year of enrolment). Please click 'Read More' below for a full list of Government Primary Schools

Seven of Grand Cayman's eight government primary schools now have a Kindergarten/Reception year; leaving Red Bay Primary School, as the only government primary school that starts students in Grade 1, at the age of five (must be five by August 31st of the year of enrolment).

In Cayman Brac, West End Primary and Creek Primary both have kindergarten years. Therefore, children who are four by September 1st can start in kindergarten (the same as the private schools) and stay in the primary school system until the end of Year 6 (aged 10, turning

11). The academic year for government schools starts at the end of Aug/start of Sept and runs through to the beginning of July.

Bodden Town Primary School

6 Condor Road, Bodden Town, Grand Cayman

Tel: +1 345 947 2288

Email: june.elliott@gov.ky

Creek Infant School (Brac)

28 Student Drive, Creek, Cayman Brac

Tel: +1 345 948 0226

Email: claudette.lazzari@gov.ky

East End Primary School

17 Sea View Road, East End, Cayman Islands.

Tel: +1 345 947 7428

Email: allison.greaves@gov.ky

Edna M. Moyle Primary School

907 North Side Road, North Side, Grand Cayman

Tel: +1 345 947 9516

Email: marcia.rennie@gov.ky

George Town Primary School

Tel: +1 345 949 2689

Email: Marie.Martin@gov.ky

John A. Cumber Primary School

44 Fountain Road, West Bay, Grand Cayman

Tel: +1 345 949 3314 Email: lorna.lumsden@gov.ky

Public High Schools

As far as public high schools go, there are three government high schools in the Cayman Islands: Two in Grand Cayman (Clifton Hunter High School in Frank Sound and John Gray High School on Academy Way in George Town), and one in Cayman Brac (the Layman E. Scott Snr. High School).

Clifton Hunter and John Gray serve Years 7-11 for students aged 11 to 16, while Layman Scott serves Years 7-12, for students aged 11 to 17. In addition, Clifton Hunter and John Gray students complete a mandatory Year 12 either at the CIFEC (Cayman Islands Further Education Centre), UCCI or at a private school where they do A Levels.

For those leaving a Government high school at the age of 16 who would like to further their education so that they can go to university there are a number of courses available at the CI Further Education Centre. Alternatively, students can apply for a scholarship to go to one of the private high schools to take A Levels or the IB programme. For colleges and universities, see our Tertiary Education section.

As far as public high schools go, there are three government high schools in the Cayman Islands:

Two in Grand Cayman (Clifton Hunter High School in Frank Sound and John Gray High Schoolon Academy Way in George Town), and one in Cayman Brac (the Layman E. Scott Snr. High School).

Curriculum

Students in government schools follow the Cayman Islands National Curriculum up to Year 9. In Year 10, students begin their preparation for internationally accredited external examinations, following the relevant syllabuses, taking exams set either by a UK exam board (GCSE/IGCSE) or the Caribbean Examinations Council (CXC) in the summer of Year 11. All students take classes in the core subjects of English, Maths, Science, Physical Education and Careers and then have the option of taking a multitude of other subjects of their choice. A minimum of five A*-C passes, including Maths and English, are considered necessary for entry to an A Level programme and ultimately to university, and are essential if applying for a government scholarship.

A very useful website for parents and students at government schools is www.des.edu.ky. It lists general information on each school, offering some incredibly detailed information on each subject's curriculum, making it a valuable resource for anyone wanting to ensure that they stay on top of their studies and have the best chance of achieving favourable exam results.

Public High Schools List

All three government high schools follow the Cayman Islands National Curriculum from years 7-9 and do CXC or GCSE from years 10-11. Access the list address below for full list of all public high schools. Clifton Hunter and John Gray serve Years 7-11 for students aged 11 to 16, while Layman Scott serves Years 7-12, for students aged 11 to 17. In addition, Clifton Hunter and John Gray students complete a mandatory Year 12 either at the CIFEC (Cayman Islands Further Education Centre), UCCI or at a private school where they do A Levels.

CI Further Education Centre (CIFEC)

515 Walkers Road, George Town, Grand Cayman

Tel: +1 345 949 3285. Email: Delores.Thompson@gov.ky

Clifton Hunter High School

311 Frank Sound Road, Frank Sound, Grand Cayman

Tel: +1 345 949 9488. Email: pauline.beckford@gov.ky

John Gray High School

73 Academy Way, George Town, Grand Cayman

Tel: +1 345 949 9444. Email: john.clark@gov.ky

Layman E. Scott High School (Brac)

941 A Dennis Foster Road, Cayman Brac

Tel: +1 345 948 2226. Email: adrian.jones@gov.ky

Exam Fees

It is worth noting that whilst all education is free for Caymanians (at government schools), parents are still liable to pay for exam entry fees. This means that they have to pay for every CXC, GCSE or BTEC course (British and Technology Education Council) that is taken. Fees are approximately CI$25 per subject for CXCs, CI$50 per GCSE and between CI$110 and $250 per BTEC Vocational Qualification, depending on the subject and the level.

Graduation Rules

To graduate with a High School Diploma, all students leaving a Government high school must attain one of four academic levels.

In addition, during their last three years (Years 10-12) they must have at least a 90% or more attendance record, along with less than 15 days of suspension. According to education officials, the aim in standardising the graduation criteria is to recognise and inspire excellence in achievement, and to make clear to both students and future employers what academic level has been attained at high school. It also helps everyone in the community understand how qualifications are ranked, and how they then match up to skills and knowledge levels. The new graduation standards will also have an important added benefit for lifelong learners, who will now have a route to gain a graduation diploma or improve the level of their diploma, once they meet the required standards. The different levels are as follows:

Level 2 diploma with high honours:

at least 9 subjects passed at Level 2 or higher, at grades I-II/A-B or the equivalent standard (grades I or II for CXC, CSEC, A*, A, or B for GCSE/IGCSE; Level 2 BTEC qualifications with Distinction; or the equivalent standard for other externally awarded qualifications) must include English and Mathematics

Level 2 diploma with honours:

at least 7 subjects passed at Level 2 or higher (i.e. grades I III for CXC, CSEC; A*-C for GCSE/IGCSE; Level 2 BTEC; or the equivalent standard for other externally awarded qualifications) must include English and Mathematics

Level 2 diploma:

at least 5 subjects passed at Level 2 or higher (i.e. grades I III for CXC, CSEC; A*-C for GCSE/IGCSE; Level 2 BTEC; or the equivalent standard for other externally awarded qualifications) must include English and Mathematics

Level 1 diploma:

at least 5 subjects passed at Level 1 or higher (e.g. grades IV-VI for CXC, CSEC, D-G for GCSE/CXC, Level 1 BTEC; or the equivalent standard for other externally awarded qualifications) must include English or Literacy Functional Skills, and Mathematics, Numeracy or Mathematics Functional Skills.

For those who then go on to Level 3 (International Baccalaureate or Advanced Placement diplomas, 'A' Levels or an Associates degree at UCCI) after leaving high school, the passing of this level indicates suitability for pursuing tertiary education.

Options for Year 12 Students

Students attending a government high school have various options for their 12th and final year of high school.

Students who have earned at least five external exam passes (CXC/GCSE/IGCSE) inclusive of Maths and English, with a grade of no less than III/C, are given "Dual Enrolment" approval for Year 12 of high school. Dual enrolment gives the Year 12 student the opportunity to either enrol at UCCI, or participate in an A Level programme at a local private school (as discussed on the previous page). Year 12 Dual Enrolment students at UCCI, have the opportunity to complete their last year of high school, while obtaining college credit towards an Associates degree. Government high school students that do not achieve five external exam passes in Year 11, are given alternative options at CIFEC for Year 12.

At CIFEC, students have the opportunity to re-sit certain external exams which they may not have passed, engage in internships and work experience and enrol in BTEC qualification programmes. Students who do not have the minimum five external passes after graduating from high school may have the opportunity to be admitted to UCCI's Pre-College Matriculation programme. This programme allows students the opportunity to take foundation level courses in Maths, English and College Skills in order to prepare students to transition into an Associates degree programme. Students can also obtain some transferable college credits in the pre-college programme

Literacy in Government Schools

An independent charitable organization called LIFE Ltd. (Literacy is for Everyone) has been set up to try to significantly improve the literacy levels in the government schools in Cayman.

They are looking for volunteers for their weekly one-to-one paired reading sessions. If you have 30 minutes per week and want to make a significant difference in a child's life and in Cayman, then email: volunteer@life.org.ky for an application form. LIFE also has a book donation programme and runs fun literacy events in the community. For further information call (345) 938 6300 or visit www.life.org.ky.

Private Education & Courses

Cayman also has quite a few private preschools, and then just a handful of private primary and high schools. As far as nurseries and preschools are concerned, remember to enrol your wee ones early! New arrivals to the island are often shocked at how quickly private schools can get filled up here - and you don't want to get stuck without a place in a school for your child.

Nurseries & Preschools

Most of the schools featured in this section accept children from newborn to four years nine months of age, offering full-day programmes and half-day options. Children will traditionally begin

Kindergarten (UK system) or a Pre-K class (US system) of their chosen primary school, in the year in which they turn five.

If you intend to send your child to one of Cayman's private primary schools and you are offered a place in their Kindergarten or Pre-K class (i.e. the reception year), you are strongly advised to take it. Keeping your child back in preschool so that they miss this first year at primary school has significant consequences: a) firstly, your child will be assessed by the primary school before they are offered a place in Year 1, to see if they are up to par with the school's expectations for a five year old (many fail this test and are not accepted) b) children at primary school start learning to read in earnest in Kindergarten and those who have not started in their preschool may feel behind in Year 1; c) your child's new classmates may have already made firm friends among the students; d) adjusting to "big school" and its lack of freedom (to play and choose what you want to work on) can be challenging for some children, and they will have missed the transition with other children in the same boat; e) on average, only five places become available in Year 1 at the top private primary schools, which means that the chances of your child being offered a place are slim at best.

As one very much-loved owner of a pre-school once said, "The role of pre-school is to allow abundant social outlet, to stimulate the imagination, to bake, create, problem solve, perform, to laugh, to form friendships, to plant, to build wigwams, to run, to climb and to be free. Cayman society places quite some pressure and elevated expectations on the academic performance of such young people, and in turn on the institutions entrusted to care for/educate them. Children develop in greatly varying time frames, and we must trust the system and trust that our children will learn each skill of physical, intellectual, linguistic, emotional and social readiness in their own good time".

If your child's preschool covers such things as the correct pencil grip and the phonetic sound of the alphabet, then this is a bonus and will definitely help your child transition to reading and writing, but if they don't, then your child's primary school will teach them these things and it should not be cause for concern. Most of the primary and high schools which have Kindergarten and Pre-K classes are listed under the Primary Schools section. Below are the majority of Cayman's preschools.

Improving Standards in Preschools

In 2013, the Ministry of Education's Early Childhood Care and Education Unit began conducting inspections of all Early Childhood Care and Education (ECCE) Centres. Their goal was to introduce new national standards and a national curriculum, for young pre-school children, ultimately shifting the schooling culture from one of child minding to one of child learning, so that children were better prepared for their entry into primary school at the age of four. The new standards not only included health and safety regulations but also how the staff were managed, how they interacted with the children and ensured that the children were being properly stimulated and taught age appropriate activities. Teachers were also taught how to identify children who might have learning difficulties and then how to better help the child so that they will be better ready for primary school.

This process is now ongoing and every preschool is inspected prior to their licence being renewed. If the school is not up to the required standard, then a three months' period of improvement is given and, as was the case in 2015, if the school did not improve then it was closed down.

The Government has chosen to focus on preschool education in an effort to address the problems in the public school system with reading, writing and behavioural issues. Therefore, to ensure that all children have access to Early Years learning, there is funding available for families on lower incomes. In order to qualify, children must be three years old as of 1st September and meet specified financial criteria. For more information and to see how to apply, see the

Department of Education Services (DES) website on www.education.gov.ky.

Here is a quick overview of all the preschools in Grand Cayman. Much much more information can be found in the listings below, but to give you a quick idea of costs and hours that the preschools are open see here:

Bright Start Learning Centre
Hours: Monday-Friday 7.30am-6pm. Playroom open Saturdays 9am-6pm
Monthly Fees: Full-day CI$660, half-day CI$475

Cayman Casa Montessori
Monthly Fees: Nest Program (4 months-16/18 months) CI$1200, Toddler Half-Day CI$900 (7.30am-12pm), Toddler Full-Day CI$1,075 (7.30am-3.30pm), Preschool Casa Half-Day CI$875 (7.30am-12.15pm), Preschool Casa Full-Day CI$1,000 (7.30am-3.30pm). Aftercare available from 3.30pm-4pm for CI$15 per day.

Discovery Kids Preschool
Hours: 7am-5.30pm
Fees: Part-time CI$400, full-time CI$550

First Baptist Christian School/WEE Care Centre
School hours: 7.30am-5.30pm (full-time), 7.30am-12.30pm (part-time)

Monthly Fees: Full-time: CI$730; Part-time (5 half-days): CI$590; Three Full Days: CI$590

Launch Pad Enrichment Centre

Hours: 6.30am-6.30pm

Monthly Fees: Full-time CI$500, half-days CI$350. After-school homework help and creative activities are available from 3pm-6.30pm for other school children Monthly CI$200. Pick-up service from Prospect Primary, Savannah Primary and Bodden Town Primary schools for an additional CI$20-40 per month. Siblings discounts available.

Little Trotters Farm & Nursery School

Hours: 7.30am-5.30pm

Monthly Fees: Half-day CI$825 (7.30am-12.30pm), full-day CI$995

Montessori Del Sol

Hours: 7.45am-3.30pm

Monthly Fees: Toddler Programme (18 months–3 years): Mornings (7.45am–11.45pm) CI$925, Toddler Extended Morning (7.45am-12.30pm) CI$995, Casa Programme (3–6 years): Montessori Mornings (7.45am–12pm) CI$885, Lunch Bunch (7.45am-1.30pm) CI$940, Full-Day (7.45am–3.30pm) CI$975. After Care (3.30pm-4.30pm) CI$15 per da. One time only application fee of CI$200. Annual registration and supplies fee CI$250.

Montessori School of Cayman

Hours: 7.30am-12.30pm (Half Days); 7.30am-3.30pm (Full Days)

Monthly Fees: Three Half Days CI$600 per month; Three Full Days CI$700 per month; Four Half Days CI$750 per month; Four Full Days CI$850 per month; Five Half Days CI$850 per month; Five Full Days -CI$925 per month.

St. George's Anglican Preschool

Hours: 7.30am-5.30pm Monday-Friday

Fees: Monthly CI$450; Fortnightly CI$250; Weekly CI$125

St. Ignatius Catholic School/Early Years Centre

Fees: Annual: CI$8,905, Per Term: CI$3,118 (3 terms) and Monthly: CI$974 (10 months)

Shining Stars Childhood Care & Education Centre

Hours: Monday-Friday 7am-6pm

Monthly Fees: CI$650 (full-time), CI$495 (part-time), CI$725 (nursery/ages 6-12 mths)

Sister Janice Early Learning Centre

Hours: 7am-6pm

Monthly Fees: CI$475 includes breakfast, lunch and afternoon snack (five Full-Days).

Sprogs Nursery and Eco-School

Monthly Fees: CI$520-CI$1,195 (depending on the number of days per week and age of the child)

Starfish Village Toddler Programme

Hours: 8am-11.30am or 8am-3pm

Monthly Fees: 3 mornings per week CI$590, 3 Full-Days per week CI$690, 5 mornings per week CI$850, 5 Full-Days per week CI$950.

The Achievement Center

Hours: 7am-6pm

Monthly Fees: CI$550 for full-time, including breakfast and lunch.

Tiny Tots Academy

Hours: 7am -6pm

Monthly Fees: 5 Full-Days (ages 6 weeks to 18 months) CI$725 per month, 5 Full-Days (19 months to 4 years) CI$675 per month. Part-time rates vary from CI$200 to CI$575 per month depending on age and the number of days attended per week. Fees include breakfast, a hot lunch and an afternoon snack.

Treasure Garden Preschool

Hours: 7.30 am-5.30pm

Monthly Fees: Full-day rate (7.30am–5.30pm) CI$850, Half-day rate (7.30am–12.30pm or 12.30pm-5.30pm) CI$700

Village Montessori

Hours: 7.30am-3.30pm

Toddler Programme Monthly Fees: (18 months-3 years) Montessori Mornings (7.30am-11.45am) CI$935 and Lunch Bunch (7.30am-1pm) CI$995

Casa Programme Monthly Fees: (3-5 years) Montessori Mornings (7.30am-12.15pm) CI$900, Lunch Bunch (7.30am-1pm) CI$950, Full-Day (7.30am-3.30 pm) CI$995.

Bright Start Learning Centre

7 Mile Shops, West Bay Road, Grand Cayman

Bright Start takes children from ages 6 weeks to 5 years of age.

Tel: +1 345 949 3017. Email: brightstartmail@gmail.com

Cayman Casa Montessori

491 Crewe Road, George Town, Grand Cayman

Cayman Casa Montessori accepts children from 4 months to 4 years of age.

Tel: +1 345 943 5846. Email: caymancasamontessori@gmail.com

Cayman International School

95 Minerva Drive, Camana Bay, Grand Cayman

Cayman International School accepts children from 2 years to 18 years.

Tel: +1 345 945 4664. Email: cis@cayintschool.kywww.caymaninternationalschool.org

Discovery Kids Preschool

Sigma Building, 93 Hospital Road, George Town, Grand Cayman

Discovery Kids accepts children from 6 weeks to 5 years of age.

Tel: +1 345 946 5437. Email: dkids.ky@gmail.com

First Baptist Christian School /WEE Care Centre

920 Crewe Road (Red Bay area), Grand Cayman

Wee Care accepts babies from 3 months, to children of 4 years and 9 months of age.

Tel: +1 345 949 0691. Email: weecare@fbcs.edu.kyweecare.edu.ky

Grace Christian Academy

21 Crescent Close, off Boltins Ave, West Bay, Grand Cayman

Grace Christian Academy accepts children from 3 years to 18 years of age.

Tel: +1 345 945 0899. Email: officeadmin@gca.ky

Launch Pad Enrichment Centre

1866 Shamrock Road, Savannah, Grand Cayman

Launch Pad accepts children from 6 weeks to 4 years 9 months.

Tel: +1 345 945 1866. Email: launchpadcayman@gmail.com

Little Trotters Farm & Nursery School

39 Columbus Close, off Walkers Road, George Town, Grand Cayman

Little Trotters accepts children from 18 months to 5 years.

Tel: +1 345 949 4080. Email: littletrotters@candw.ky

Montessori by The Sea

277 Prospect Point Drive, Prospect, Grand Cayman

Montessori By The Sea accepts children from 21 months to 14 years old.

Tel: +1 345 947 0684. Email: kourtni@mbts.kywww.mbts.ky

Montessori Del Sol

11 Hinds Way, off Walkers Road, George Town, Grand Cayman

Montessori Del Sol accepts children aged 18 months to 6 years.

Tel: +1 345 949 3222Email: montessori@candw.ky

Montessori School of Cayman

519 South Church Street, George Town, Grand Cayman

Montessori School of Cayman accepts children aged 18 months to 4 years and 9 months.

Tel: +1 345 949 0202. Email: montessorischoolofcayman@gmail.com

Shining Stars

17 Pasadora Place, Pines Road, Off Smith Road (near the George Town Hospital).

Shining Stars accepts children from 6 weeks to 5 years of age

Tel: +1 345 943 7077. Email: shiningstarscayman@gmail.com

www.shiningstarscayman.com

Sister Janice Early Learning Centre

41 Desmond Drive, off Crewe Rad, George Town, Grand Cayman

Sister Janice's accepts children aged 6 months to 5 years.

Tel: +1 345 949 2524. Email: sisterjanicepreschool@yahoo.com

St. George's Anglican Preschool

64 Courts Road, Off Eastern Avenue, George Town, Grand Cayman

St. George's accepts children aged 2 years to 5 years.

Tel: +1 345 945 0441. Email: stgeorgespreschool@candw.ky

St. Ignatius Catholic School

599 Walkers Road, George Town, Grand Cayman

Sr. Ignatius accepts children from 3 years to 18 years of age.

Tel: +1 345 949 9250. Email: general@st-ignatius.com

www.st-ignatius.com/

Starfish Village Toddler Programme

94 Solaris Avenue, Camana Bay, Grand Cayman

Starfish Village Toddler Programme accepts children from 2 to 4 years.
Tel: +1 345 938 7464. Email: info@starfish.ky

The Achievement Center

295 Shamrock Road, next to Red Bay Primary, Grand Cayman

The Achievement Center accepts children from 12 months to 4 years 9 months.

Tel: +1 345 947 5050. Email: achieve4u@hotmail.com

Tiny Tots Academy

109 Hinds Way, off Walkers Road, George Town, Grand Cayman

Tiny Tots accepts children from ages 6 weeks to 4 years 11 months.

Tel: +1 345 623 8687. Email: tinytotsacademy.ky@gmail.com

Treasure Garden Preschool

19 Pond Road, off Smith Road, George Town, Grand Cayman

Treasure Garden Preschool accepts children from 18 months to 5 years.

Tel: +1 345 943 6230 Email: treasuregardenpreschool@hotmail.com

www.treasuregardenpreschool.com

Village Montessori

94 Solaris Avenue, Camana Bay, Grand Cayman

Village Montessori accepts children aged 18 months to 6 years.

Tel: +1 345 938 7464. Email: villagemontessori@starfish.ky

Kindergarten, Primary & High Schools

Cayman has a good selection of excellent private schools, each following either the British or American curriculum.

In both systems the main student intake is for Kindergarten (British) and Pre-K (US). The most popular schools have very few places available in Year 1, so think carefully if you are offered a place and decide to delay your child's entry for a year. Students can then remain in their chosen school up to Year 13 (UK system) and Year 12 (US system).

Schools following the UK system take GCSEs and A Levels and the US system offers either the IB programme or prepares students to take the Scholastic Aptitude Test (SAT) and attain a US High School Diploma. Exam results have been phenomenal with students in the UK system, each gaining on average 10 GCSEs and 3 A Levels, with passes from A to C

Cayman Academy

Cayman Academy accepts children from 2 years 9 months to 16 years. Tel: +1 345 640 2630. Email: caymanacademyschool@gmail.com www.cayman.academy

Cayman International School

95 Minerva Drive, Camana Bay, Grand Cayman

Cayman International School accepts children from 2 years to 18 years.

Tel: +1 345 945 4664. Email: cis@cayintschool.ky

www.caymaninternationalschool.org

Cayman Prep & High School

A private primary and high school (on two separate campuses) in George Town, Grand Cayman which accepts boys and girls from ages 4 to 18.

Tel: +1 345 949 9115. Email: psoffice@cayprep.edu.ky

www.cayprep.edu.ky

First Baptist Christian School

920 Crewe Road, Red Bay, Grand Cayman

FBCS accepts children from ages 5 to 12 years.

Tel: +1 345 945 7906. Email: fbcs@fbcs.edu.ky

www.fbcs.edu.ky

Grace Christian Academy

21 Crescent Close, off Boltins Ave, West Bay, Grand Cayman

Grace Christian Academy accepts children from 3 years to 18 years of age.

Tel: +1 345 945 0899. Email: officeadmin@gca.ky

Hope Academy

Units 1-8 Grand Harbour Shoppes, Red Bay, Grand Cayman

Hope Academy accepts children from ages 5 to 18 years.

Tel: +1 345 769 4673. Email: office@hopecayman.com

www.hopecayman.com

Montessori by The Sea

277 Prospect Point Drive, Prospect, Grand Cayman

Montessori By The Sea accepts children from 21 months to 14 years old.

Tel: +1 345 947 0684. Email: kourtni@mbts.ky

www.mbts.ky

St. Ignatius Catholic School

599 Walkers Road, George Town, Grand Cayman

Sr. Ignatius accepts children from 3 years to 18 years of age.

Tel: +1 345 949 9250 Email: general@st-ignatius.com

www.st-ignatius.com/

Triple C School

74 Fairbanks Road, George Town, Grand Cayman

Triple C School accepts children from ages 4 years to 17 years.

Tel: +1 345 949 6022. Email: triplec@candw.ky

www.triplecschool.org/

Truth for Youth School

84 Walkers Road, George Town, Grand Cayman

Truth For Youth accepts children from 4 years 9 moths to 11 years of age.

Tel: +1 345 949 2620. Email: truthfys@candw.ky

Wesleyan Christian Academy

150 North West Point Road, West Bay, Grand Cayman

Wesleyan Christian Academy accepts students from age 3 years 9 months to 18 years.

Tel: +1 345 949 1121. Email: principal@wcacayman.com

Home Schooling

According to the Cayman Islands Department of Education Services, persons who are legally resident in the Cayman Islands who wish to home school their children may do so with the approval of the Department of Education Services.

Children in the Cayman Islands can be home schooled with prior approval from the Department of Education Services. In 2017, 115 children were enrolled in home schooling programmes in Cayman. Like any educational programme, there is an application process and certain requirement to be met, which are discussed below, along with an overview of the advantages, disadvantages and resources available for home schoolers.

Home Schooling May be a Suitable Option in Cases Where:

> A child is wait listed but has not yet been offered a place in a private school

> A child has learning difficulties that schools may not have the resources to deal with

> The cost of private schooling is prohibitive for low income families and/or those with multiple children

> Families travel frequently and wish to be able to take their children with them

> A child has been the victim of bullying at school

Parents wishing to home school their child/children must obtain prior approval from the Department of Education Services.

To Apply for Home Schooling Approval:

Complete the Home School Registration Form. This can be downloaded from www.des.edu.ky, under the School Registration tab.

Create an **Individualized Home School Plan (IHSP)**. This must include:

1. The child's name, age and grade level
2. Location and address of the home school
3. A list of the syllabi, curriculum materials, textbooks, or plan of

instruction to be used in the core subjects

4. The dates for submission of semi-annual reports

5. Names and qualifications of individuals providing instruction

6. A statement confirming the child will be meeting compulsory educational requirements of Education Law 2010

7. These must be submitted along with a cover letter explaining the reasons for the home schooling request to the Director of the Department of Education Services at 130 Thomas Russell Avenue, PO Box 91, KY1-1103, Grand Cayman.

Applications must be made by August 1st of each school year. For parents wishing to apply after the start of the school year (end August) written notice must be provided within 14 days. The Chief Education Officer will inform parents if their application has been approved within 10 days of receipt. If approved, a home school certificate is issued, valid for one year. This must be renewed prior to expiration each year if the parent wishes to continue home schooling.

A home school cannot serve more than five students.

Qualifications for Home Schoolers

Depending on the age of the child, the parent or tutor providing instruction must hold the following qualifications:

Primary the parent(s) must have at least a high school diploma.

Secondary the parent/tutor must be a licensed teacher with a minimum of a bachelor's degree from an accredited institution.

Online programs accredited programs such as K12 have online teachers.

Teaching Requirements

The DES requires that the school day be at least five hours, excluding recess and lunch, and that there be at least 185 days of instruction in the school year.

The curriculum must include the areas of reading, writing, mathematics, sciences and social studies, and must be an accredited programme. Parents/tutors must maintain a record of attendance and submit semi-annual reports on the students' progress to the Department of Education.

The DES will conduct at least two site visits, one scheduled, one impromptu each year. More information on the pros and cons of home schooling in Cayman and also useful resources for home schoolers can be found on our website.

Pros & Cons of Home Schooling

The main advantages home schooling parents report is being able to spend more time with their children and having the ability to adapt the teaching to a child's learning style, ensuring they receive a quality education and plenty of individual attention.

The flexibility home schooling offers is also key: classes can be held in any location, and at the time one chooses, enabling parents to fit schooling around other commitments.

On the other hand, homeschooling is time-consuming for the parent (or tutor) providing instruction, and thus means that one parent usually cannot work, and therefore cannot contribute to the family's income. It also means the 'teaching' parent may get little or no time apart from their children.

Socialisation & Friendship for Home Schooled Children

One of the most frequently asked questions that parents, who home school their children, get asked is whether there is a danger that a child who is home schooled might miss out on socialising with their age group and thus have less friends than a regular school goer? It's a valid concern, but there is much that can be done to ensure a child does not become isolated.

Enrolling kids in extra curricular activities, sports lessons, church groups, music and art lessons, all ensure they meet and socialise with kids of their age. Where one lives can also be influential: some residential areas are particularly family friendly, guaranteeing there will be plenty of other kids around to play with.

The CaymanHomeschoolers facebook group was set up specifically so that parents and children could connect with other homeschooling friends. These children go on field trips with other parents and children and time is specifically set aside each week to socialize with the other kids. A homeschooling family can become just as busy with extra curricular activities as any other public/private school family.

Resources for Cayman Homeschoolers

In addition to numerous online resources for both curricula and general advice and recommendations for home schooling, Cayman has its own community resource, Cayman Homeschoolers, established by Tiffany Knowles. There is both a public page and private group on Facebook (CaymanHomeschoolers) where local homeschoolers can make contact, ask questions, share ideas and plan events and field trips.

A growing number of after school programmes, both academic and non-academic, offer options for homeschooled students to participate in.

Footsteps provides home schooling support in individual, paired or group sessions, either for odd hours, or covering whole subject areas.

Clever Fish works alongside the home schooling community and offers an after school enrichment programme, that includes homework supervision, academic intervention and activities such as robotics, arts and crafts and more. They also offer activity camps in collaboration with Cayman Sea Elements during school holidays.

Overseas Education & Boarding Schools

Although Cayman has excellent schools, many parents will look to broaden their children's horizons by sending them to overseas boarding schools.

Although Cayman has excellent schools, many parents will look to broaden their children's horizons by sending them to overseas boarding schools. Over the years the image of boarding schools has changed immeasurably; the transformation from the hardship and coldness of Dickens' Dotheboys Hall to the spellbinding excitement of Hogwarts has been both evolutionary and revolutionary. However, the changes in perception and the reality are not works of fiction; boarding schools in Britain and North America are flourishing and should be a real consideration for families thinking about the future schooling of their children. But what makes a boarding school education special?

1. **First Rate Education**

   The reputation of leading schools in the UK, USA and Canada is not just a label of prestige from the past; the academic, sporting and social success of these schools is in the present and the future. Academic excellence, their successes in international exams and their students winning places at Ivy League and Russell Group universities speak for themselves. The structured independence helps teenagers to thrive.

2. **All-Round Education**

   Boarding schools are concerned with much more than academic prowess; pupils exceeding their potential in the classroom is paramount, of course, but the ability to be involved in whichever sporting, creative or intellectual pursuit that stimulates a child, is of huge importance too. All these things are on the student's doorstep; schools are extremely busy places where children are seldom bored or lonely and, rather charmingly, it is still seen to be cool to do something rather than nothing.

3. **Support**

   Success is achieved through sound teaching and individual care and attention. Staff at boarding schools are with their students twenty-four hours a day and are there to ensure that every child is happy and performing well at all times, addressing problems swiftly. Boarding schools are well-equipped and qualified to support most learning requirements and a wide range of schools offer specialist Additional Support for learning and emotional needs.

4. **Facilities**

Boarding schools have some outstanding facilities and offer beautiful spaces in which youngsters can grow and develop. Academic and sporting facilities can be state-of-the-art, and boarding houses are often not far shy of a reasonable hotel.

5. **Friends**

Whilst boarding school pupils can no longer rely on the 'old school tie' to garner success in later life, a boarding education exposes youngsters to a huge array of people some they will become life-long friends with, others they will get to know well, but they will probably know these people better than they know anyone else in their lives. The ability to live and work with such a huge number of people is what gives boarding school students the confidence and maturity to excel in their future worlds. Exposure to the wider world and internationalism also helps prepare students for the world of business.

6. **Finance**

    Boarding school fees can seem eye-wateringly expensive fees can be as high as £32,000 or US$59,000 a year. However, boarding schools are working increasingly hard to ensure that they are not 'elitist' and seek to attract the students who will most benefit from all the school has to offer. It is always worth asking about Bursary and Scholarship assistance.

Choosing The Right Boarding School

The process of selecting the right school for your children can be something of a minefield. Niall Browne, of BvS Education, and a seasoned former independent school teacher, offers some pointers:

1. **Find the right school for your child**

    It is vital to find the school in which your child will be happy and will thrive. Friends and acquaintances may offer school suggestions based on their own children's success (or otherwise!) but, just because this school was right for their children, is no guarantee that it will be right for yours. Choose a school based on your child's talents, interests and needs, even if this is wildly different to that chosen by others. Unless your child is happy and comfortable at their new school, they won't perform well in the classroom or the rugby pitch. Make sure that the school offers the qualifications (International Baccalaureate; GCSE; A Level;

SATs; Vocational courses) best suited to your child and their intended higher education and career path.

2. **Don't be a slave to League Tables**

    League Tables, inspections reports and reputation only tell a very small part of the story and are often flawed. Only by visiting a school will you be able to see whether or not it measures up academically, if its facilities appeal to your child and the staff and pupils are warm and engaging. Just like buying a house: you either like the décor and feel of a house as a future home, or you don't regardless of how wonderful the market thinks it is or isn't.

3. **Time & Preparation**

    The world of independent education is as competitive as any walk of life and many schools fill their places several years in advance of entry. Therefore, give yourself plenty of time time to choose the right school, time to visit, time for your child to be prepared for the entrance exams and for the transition to boarding school. Parents often underestimate how much time should be given to these steps, but at least one or two years in advance is the best time to begin the process. If you are still undecided about whether to send your child to school in the UK or North America, go through the process you do not have to commit to anything at the exploratory stages.

4. **Getting help**

    There are many people who can advise you about UK or North American independent schools, and it is worth seeking guidance this is, after all, one of the most important decisions you will make for your child. However, it is important to choose a consultant who really knows the full range of British or North American independent schools and the complicated admission procedures involved. Find an expert rather than a gifted amateur.

5. **Enjoy the process**

    You will potentially be visiting some of the finest schools in the world and giving your child untold opportunities and experiences in fact you may actually wish you were going in their place!

School Fairs

Two school fairs take place in Grand Cayman each year offering parents the opportunity to meet representatives from various overseas boarding schools.

British Schools Fair, Cayman Islands

The British School Fair is usually held during the middle weekend in September each year, but the school representatives often stay in

Cayman on either side of this weekend and are happy to conduct interviews or answer any questions that parents may have. For more information, contact Niall Browne of BvS Education on info@bvs-education.com or visit www.bvs-education.co.uk/british-schools-fairs.

Caribbean School Fair

The Caribbean School Fair which is run by Bedi Walker of Educational Consulting & School Placement Services, is usually held the third weekend in November at the Marriott Hotel Grand Cayman and between 30 and 40 of Canada's and the USA's top boarding schools attend. For a list of the attending schools please email Bedi Walker on info@bediwalker.com.

Modestus Hopkins